UNTANGLED

Henry J. Sienkiewicz

First published by Dog Ear Publishing
4010 W. 86th Street, Ste H
Indianapolis, IN 46268
www.dogearpublishing.net

ISBN:978-1-4575-1826-3

This book is printed on acid-free paper.

Printed in the United States of America

To Jeffrey

Contents

List of Illustrations

CHAPTER 1

Just Around the Bend

All journeys have secret destinations
of which the traveler is unaware.

—Martin Buber

*W*e were a boisterous bunch as we began our hike across the island of Taiwan. A group of Scouts and a few adult leaders, we were all set and ready to go. Our backpacks were neatly packed. Our ropes were rolled and stored. With everything planned and equipment on hand, we could start.

The beginning of the journey

From the beginning, we were surrounded by spectacular scenery. To the north, we saw mountain peaks; to the south, we saw another set of mountain peaks. In between were a series of beautiful canyons, pristine rivers, and picture-perfect farms. Our journey was to be through this fantastic scene into the heart of the island.

The region was formed starting millions of years ago. After the initial collision of tectonic plates, the beauty underlying it all was slowly exposed through erosion and cultivation.

Emergence continues here to this day as the landscape continues to be transformed by both man and nature. What is emerging is an impressive but daunting landscape. Like a classical Chinese painting which boldly and in detail depicts towering mountains, rolling hills, and rushing rivers, it is one of the most beautiful areas in the world.

What compelled us to leave our homes and to take this journey?

Human history is replete with stories about journeys and wanderings. The Buddha wandered. The Bible begins with human expulsion and subsequent wandering. *The Odyssey* was a tale about wandering. Moses was condemned to wander. Dorothy journeyed to Oz.

It is in our nature to journey. We are a nomadic people, and it is in our nature to want to experience and comprehend the world around us.

What did we expect to get from our journey?

We can choose to simply leave home and come back without any significant change. We can compact our journeys, we can take packaged tours in air-conditioned tour buses, and we can be merely entertained as we drive by the sights. We can pretend and falsely believe that we have engaged in a meaningful journey.

Our journeys do not necessarily promise transformation. Our journeys have no inherent moral character. Our journeys do not necessarily have to have any outcomes. Our journeys are only as good as what we offer of ourselves in the process. We can choose to not see the beauty around us. We can choose to not see the foundations of life or the pillars supporting our bridges.

We had yet to reach our first campsite, yet to unpack our tents and unroll our sleeping bags. We had left the jump-off point and were working our way along a relatively well-traveled path. We knew that we had hours and miles to go.

But the Scouts were already asking if we were at our first campsite, at our initial destination. Our response was that our destination was "just around the bend," which became a commonly heard refrain during the course of the trip and came to symbolize the emergent nature of our journey.

As we go "just around the bend," we journey to find a greater understanding. As we go "just around the bend," we journey to find a continual emergence. As we go "just around the bend," we will become entangled. As we go "just around the bend," each of us can choose to use contemplation to make sense of the journey and entanglements. As we go "just around the bend," we can see that contemplation is based in silence, stillness and solitude. As we go "just around the bend," we can repack our mental backpacks, engage the world and awaken beauty.

We are all on our own journeys, with our own trail bends. Untangling through contemplation will allow us to become engaged and make sense of the journey. Untangling lets us make intentional choices. Untangling gives us an approach by which to choose and, in turn, to make the world more understandable.

CHAPTER 2

Morning Mist

I see my path, but I don't know where it leads. Not knowing where I'm going is what inspires me to travel it.

—Rosalia de Castro

*T*he mornings started off mist laden on this two-hundred-year-old high-mountain trail. As the night ended, a light covering of mist would envelop everything. The mist was not clinging; the mist was not cloying; the mist was simply enveloping.

Early morning mountain mists

As the mist cleared, we could only get a glimmer of where we were going that day. We needed to start walking to fully see and ultimately experience the trail.

What we would find is that the trail taken by previous travelers could have washed away, and we would have to find a new one. The trail could shift in character, and we would have to rapidly transition from safe to dangerous and back to safe in a matter of yards. The trail could have completely vanished, and we would have to find our own way.

Things emerged as we traveled along. Sometimes these things were new to us; sometimes these things were truly novel. This trail was very much like our own world.

On our own journeys, our own entanglements emerge as if from the morning mist. Some trails taken by previous travelers have washed away, and we have to find new ones. Other trails are still in place, and we can pass safely. As our mist-laden entanglements clear, we see that we are in a transition point in the world.

We are at a unique place and time, with an emergence of trends that requires us to change. With an almost infinite number of entanglements in our networked society, we need to find ways to understand and cope with all of the possibilities surrounding us.

We need to pause to understand ourselves and understand where we are going. We need to break through the fear surrounding us in order to continue, even if we don't know where our journeys will lead us. We can comprehend our journeys as we find distance through cultivated contemplation.

Cultivated contemplation allows us to clear our own mists and to find the distance to understand ourselves and clearly see our trail. By allowing clarity of thought, contemplation lets us see through the strobe lights and the immediate to the perennial.

As we go along our journeys, we need to ask, what is contemplation? Why do we need it? How can we cultivate it in life?

CHAPTER 3

Nightly Embers

The universe is made of stories, not atoms.

—Muriel Rukeyser

*I*f the morning mist began our day, our nightly campfire ended it. As the campfires were lit and the day slowly came to a close, we talked about the adventures we had. We shared our stories, the stories of our days, the stories of our lives. We shared our narratives. We discussed what went right and what we could do better. And then, we let our thoughts slow down like the embers of the fire in front of us.

We were able to spend time to craft and tell our stories. I learned an important lesson a number of years ago from an organization called SpeakeasyDC. In the words of their mission statement, "Through the art of autobiographical story performance, SpeakeasyDC gives voice to the authentic experience of ordinary people, builds community, and promotes understanding." SpeakeasyDC also believes that "the stories have a narrative arc which, in a nutshell, means there are characters and a plot." Stories are not essays, jokes, or poetry.

What they taught me is that our interactions are based on the exchange of stories. As we create our narratives, we create stories about the decisions we make and the consequences that follow. Our storytelling lets us weave a narrative out of our actions and words. Our storytelling allows us to look back and comprehend the significance and importance for both ourselves and those around us.

Our narratives are highly personalized episodic movies. We expose ourselves to the listeners. Our movies have a rich texture of details so that the other person is not passive; the other is seeing what we saw, hearing what we heard, smelling what we smelled, and touching what we touched. The other person experiences what we experienced. Our narratives enrich, extend, and engage. In turn, the listeners expose themselves to themselves and to each other.

We can see that our narratives are spatially and temporally defined. We need some distance and time from the events we are describing in order to provide us with further insights.

We can also see that our lives are not an unrelated succession of independent actions or projects or states of being. Our lives have a trajectory. Since our lives have a trajectory, we can conceive it narratively.

This does not mean that a person must conceive or live his or her life narratively. One does not say, "Here is the story that I want to construct, and I have to adhere to this specific script."

Our lives can be seen as a story or, better, as a series of stories that are more or less related. We play the central role in each episode and provide the element of continuity.

In the steps of Thomas Merton and Jacques Maritain, how can we bring contemplation to our daily activities? In the spirit of Aristotle's *Ethics*, how can we cultivate the distance to create our narratives and tell our stories? How can we have the ability to slow down like the fire's embers in order to allow contemplation into our daily lives?

Contemplation is a journey toward deep self-knowledge as we share our narratives. It is not an expedition to find fault. Contemplation allows us to begin to fill in the narrative deficit in the world.

Contemplation is a process that slowly and quietly lets you untangle from the things that constrain you. I contend that our daily activities are the basis for contemplation, and in turn, contemplation is the basis for our daily activities. Each informs the other.

As you go through this journey, you may not like what you find. You may not find what you thought you were looking for. But you will find something.

By way of definition, contemplation is neither prayer nor meditation. Prayer is properly understood as having a conversation with God or the saints. Meditation is generally an internally facing personal practice. Individuals do it by and for themselves.

I'm focused on the type of contemplation traditionally referred to as "masked contemplation." Masked contemplation is the fostering of deep understanding while remaining in the active life. I am basing this on the ideas put forward by other writers such as Saint Augustine and Hannah Arendt.

In his writings, Saint Augustine mentioned three kinds of life: a life of the purely contemplative (introvert), an active life (extrovert), and a life composed of both. It is this third type of life of both contemplative and active, thoughtful yet engaged in daily activities, on which I am concentrating.

In order to do so, for most of us, the way to approach contemplation is through our daily activities. We have to cultivate contemplation so that it may occur naturally in the responsibilities, tasks, and relationships of daily life.

I don't presume to offer a set series of steps to a life of contemplation. I offer a framework that fosters and enables a life that fully integrates and respects contemplation as an essential element.

CHAPTER 4

A Big Ball of Twine

We learn the rope of life by untying its knots.

—Jean Toomer

*A*s we reached the first stopping point, we opened our packs and found chaos. The ropes that we had neatly packed were completely jumbled. The gear we had carefully stowed had been shifted around; it was an unrecognizable mess.

The jostling and shifting from the simple movement of the journey caused our coils of rope to transform from a neat roll to an entangled mess. We thought that we had taken care to pack them; the journey ensured that we had a mess to deal with.

Twine to untangle

Our mental backpacks are similar. Sometimes, regardless of the care we have taken, our world becomes a completely entangled mess in ways that we had not expected. Our journey ensures that we have a mess to deal with.

Many writers have used the terms *connected* and *hyperconnected* to describe our current state. I think that the term *entanglement* is more reflective of the state of our condition.

Connection implies that there has been an encounter but does not imply that the relationship is persistent. As will be discussed later, entanglement means two or more "things" have formed some type of permanent bond. This permanent bond is why I think that the term entanglement is more expressive of our actual condition.

Entanglement has many layers and many textures. It may be accidental or intentional. Entanglement may be in ways that may or may not be are attractive. Entanglement may or may not have relevancy to our lives. Entanglement may or may not have real meaning.

Entanglement may be the vines that catch your feet. Or it may be the limbs that brush your arms. Or it could be the rope that safely holds you onto the mountain.

Contemplation lets us mentally sort through the mess of entanglement that we all carry with us and allows us to repack meaningfully.

CHAPTER 5

Entangled

Spooky action at a distance.

—Albert Einstein

*A*s the days and miles went by, we had new experiences. These experiences surprised us. These experiences challenged us. These experiences became part of us. These experiences entangled us.

Entanglements continually happen to us. For every interaction, every moment is an opportunity for a new entanglement.

Today's world is deeply entangled economically, religiously, and socially. No significant political, spiritual, or economic trend leaves the rest of the world untouched.

We have all experienced this. We may strike up a friendship in the most unusual of places. We may learn something from the most unlikely of sources. Entanglements revolve around our relationships, our spiritual sense, our physical nature, and our careers.

Everything touches everything else. Everyone touches everyone else. All human behavior appears on the Internet and appears in ways that are both accessible and permanent. There is potential for entanglement previously denied; there is a potential for entanglement previously not imagined.

One of the interesting new developments in physics is a series of scientific experiments characterized by the overarching term *entanglement.* The premise is that when two particles of matter interact, a permanent bond is formed.

This is where it gets spooky. From then on, a connection, an entanglement, will always exist between them regardless of how far apart they are. Even at opposite ends of the universe, they will be in some state of nonseparability. Like our spools of rope, things will loosen, and things will overlap. Things go their separate ways, but at some level, they remain connected.

While not fully explained, entanglement holds that there was a point in time in which every atom in the universe was condensed into a singularity prior to expanding—in short, the big bang theory. All particles were once compacted tightly together. As a consequence, everything was connected and everything remains connected in some fashion; everything is entangled at some level.

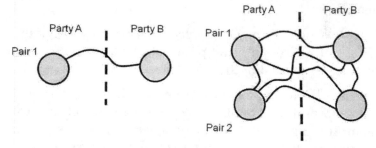

Simple entanglement: single and biparticle

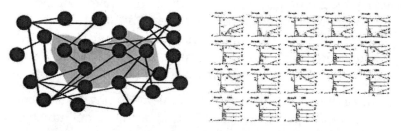

Complex entanglement: lattice and Feynman diagrams

Entanglement becomes complex very, very quickly. Simple entanglement is about simple interactions as seen in the diagrams with single and biparticle entanglements. Complex entanglement involves multiple interactions played out sequentially and over time. Highly complex entanglement is a consequence of multiple interactions, coupled with shape, time, and heritable instructions. The lattice and Feynman diagrams show visualizations of the complex interactions of entanglements.

My concern is that, with so much entanglement, we end up spending the majority of our lives losing ourselves within it. We lose ourselves within the complexity. We lose ourselves within the tree limbs. We become entertained with the immediate and don't fully engage. We never recognize the whole.

The almost infinite number of entanglements in our networked society makes the world almost impossible to understand and cope with. Untangling lets us to find ways to understand and cope with all of the possibilities surrounding us.

CHAPTER 6

Why the Chaos?

Chaos is the score upon which reality is written.

—Henry Miller

hat caused our backpacks to get so chaotic? We packed them with care. We packed them with thought. We took the time and effort to make sure that everything was in order.

The simple act of taking the journey causes entanglement. The simple act of doing anything causes our mental backpacks to become a mess.

We could choose to do nothing. We could choose to not take the journey. We could be content to stay in place and not change at all. If that is your choice, then I would suggest that you just put this book down or give it to someone else.

But I don't think that we can make that choice. We are a nomadic race; we travel, we explore, we learn, we grow. We grow by becoming entangled, then becoming untangled, in turn deciding how to become entangled again.

Our entanglements are driven primarily by two things. Entanglements are driven by love or by fear. The former takes time to develop and to cultivate. The latter is much more immediate and erosive in nature.

While we talk a great deal about love, as I have written elsewhere, it is the least understood aspect of human life. Yet love is the most compelling and most fragile aspect of human life. Fundamentally, it is what makes us human.

We all experience love in an absolutely unique manner, although love is based in one of three aspects: *phileo, eros,* or *agape.* Using the definitions I put forward in *Centerlined* that phileo love is the friendship, routinely strengthened by shared experiences. Eros is a sensual love, stimulated by our senses. Agape is a pure love, selflessly and unconditionally expressed.

Our entanglements are also driven by an obsessive focus on our fears: our fears of the past, our fears of the future, our fears of our mistakes, our fears of perceived weaknesses, or our fears of being alone. Fear is caused by our perception of a threat.

While I hold that our love entanglements are almost universally good, entanglements based in fear are not. Fear can be good, and fear can be bad. Fear arises when we ask ourselves what it is all about, but we don't have enough distance to see a deeper perspective.

Under normal circumstances, fear is not a problem. Fear is protective. Fear makes us aware of danger. Fear helps us understand the world and ourselves.

Fear can be very bad. We are often held hostage by our non-protective fears.

Fear has to do with the future. But the future does not exist. It hasn't happened yet. Fear has to do with the past. But the past has already happened.

These fears can paralyze us and cause us to do nothing. These fears can cause us to put our backs against a wall, put up our physical or mental fists, and swing and flail around. We end up being ruled by fear and those who have come to understand how to use fear to control.

An interesting way of describing fear is that fear is "False Evidence Appearing Real." Inevitably, the non-protective fears that hold us hostage have nothing to do with right now.

Acknowledging the idea that the act of taking the journey causes entanglements, we can also accept the notion that entanglements are based in either love or ear. The question that we should now ask is, "What are some of the most common entanglements?"

CHAPTER 7

What Was Entangled?

Man is a knot, a web into which relationships are tied.
Only these relationships matter.

—Antoine de Saint-Exupéry

*I*n order to make camp, we had to go into our backpacks. We pulled out the entangled coils of rope. It took us a while to sort through the mess and figure out which rope was which. We had to identify each strand and slowly unwind each.

Our lives have similar strands, which we need to slowly unwind. To try to understand what entangles us, I use the model set forth by Shakti Gawain in *Creating True Prosperity*. Gawain used four categories which, for these purposes, I'm calling the ropes of entanglement: relationships, spiritual, physical, and career. As I outlined in *Centerlined*, we need to explore each of these in depth.

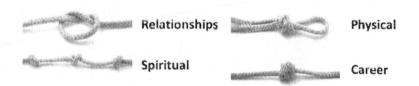

Relationships   Physical

Spiritual   Career

Ropes of entanglement

Relational ropes are the entanglements that we have with those around us—our families, our friends, our healthy relationships,

17

our unhealthy relationships, our physical relationships, our virtual relationships.

Spiritual ropes are the entanglements that we form as we discover and explore our ontological nature. What do we believe in? Is there a God? What do we profess?

Physical ropes are the entanglements that we create as we strive for mental and physical well-being and fitness. They could be the illnesses we have; they could be the pains we carry. They can be our exercise regime.

Finally, career ropes are the entanglements that we find as we embrace our professions. Do our professions give us a sense of real achievement? Do our professions provide long-term value?

These ropes continually envelop us. They are not bad. They are not good. They simply are. They are simply a part of us, and we need to understand how we react to and embrace them.

CHAPTER 8

Embracing Entanglement

Be open to your dreams, people. Embrace that distant shore.
Because our mortal journey is over all too soon.

—David Assael

As I have gotten older, my experience of, my reaction to, and my respect for entanglements has changed. I have come to better understand, trust, and actually embrace entanglements.

We have three possible methods of dealing with entanglements: *attraction*, *aversion*, and *indifference*. These are the ways in which we knowingly or unknowingly react to everything.

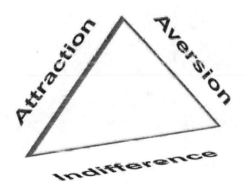

Response to entanglement

Attraction relates to those things that we should try to bring closer to ourselves. Aversions are those things that we should push away from. Indifference is the neutral state; it is neither attractive nor aversive in nature. We can be attracted to both love and fear. We can have aversion to both love and fear. We can be indifferent to both love and fear.

How do we first recognize and evaluate the entanglements? How do we decide if we want to make them part of our lives? Do we push them away? Do we simply let them lie in the background?

A possible answer is recognizing, acknowledging, and incorporating the entanglements though contemplation. What I have seen is that as my awareness and sensitivity increase to the entanglements around me, I am able to cultivate more directly the distance necessary to embrace entanglements.

CHAPTER 9

Limbs, Trees, Habitat

We cannot live only for ourselves.
A thousand fibers connect us with our fellow men.

—Herman Melville

*A*s we walked on the trail, we could see the trees in front of us. The branches slapped us in the face. The briars snagged our pant legs. We could feel our immediate entanglements. We could see our immediate entanglements. We were in the middle of them. We were surrounded by them.

We could not see how dense the forest was. We could not see its borders. We were only able to see what was immediately around us. We did not have a perspective on the whole.

It was hard to see—much less describe—the whole forest. For us, at that moment, the whole was next to impossible to recognize. It was only in the clearings that we had enough distance to see a broader perspective, although not the whole.

Limbs, trees, habitat

Our world is like that. We go about our daily activities and just see the activities, our tree limbs. We become so entangled in the daily activities and *doxa* that we just accept certain norms or approaches as "facts." By way of a simplified definition, doxa is the Greek term for "common knowledge." We accept the status quo as not just how we do things but as the only right way to do things. Contemplation helps us change the scale of our mental maps so we can step back and gain a broader perspective.

While we may have a map in our minds, we realize that sometimes a single scale does not always work. We have occasions where we want to see a higher level of detail. We have occasions where we want to see a different perspective.

We need to learn how to shift our perspectives between telescopic and microscopic perspectives, in a multiscopic fashion. No one would display a continental map in order to find a restaurant. The necessary details won't be seen. However, we don't need building blueprints to know that the restaurant is there. We need to find a way to choose the relevant scale. We need to choose to learn how to actively contemplate.

CHAPTER 10

The Waves

The breaking of a wave cannot explain the whole sea.

—Vladimir Nabokov

I relate the idea of limbs, trees and habitat to the abstract idea of dealing with the vectors of entanglement through the image of water waves. On the first leg of this journey, the group passed by one of the picturesque lakes that dot the Taiwanese countryside. While it had a placid surface, from past experiences I knew that surfaces could be deceiving. On a lake or in the ocean, waves could vastly differ.

In this analogy, there are three different types of waves in our internal lives that correspond to the limb, tree, and habitat. These are immediate, long, and underlying waves.

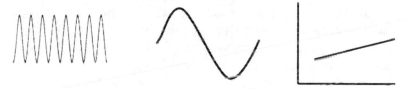

Immediate, long, and underlying waves

Our daily lives are full of immediate waves, the daily noise, the daily chores, the daily encounters. They are the limbs that hit us in the face and the vines that grab us by the ankles. Immediate waves are composed of the daily "stuff" of life. Immediate waves impact us but may not develop us. We react to them. We don't intentionally act

While frequent, the immediate waves may not be meaningful except as distractions. We believe them to be important because they are pressing upon us. In a technical sense, we commonly follow the fallacy of availability heuristic. Availability heuristic is when we judge the importance of an event based on how easily we can think of an example. We also follow the fallacy of correlation. We confuse immediacy with importance.

Our perspectives and understanding of our entanglements can be as equally myopic. The closer we are to something, the greater the weight we give it. The more details we can make out, the more likely we think a particular act will occur. The immediate and frequent entanglements appear to have great weight. We end up giving undue weight to the immediate waves.

Along with immediate waves are two others waves: long waves and what I call underlying waves. The long waves are the narrative themes in our lives. Long waves are the doxa of our society. I liken them to the trees that we can see once we have enough distance to recognize them.

The underlying waves are the habitats we are in; the underlying waves are the transcendental realities or perennial truths of life. These are the waves that are the underpinnings of reality. These are the waves that we see only infrequently. They are the vistas we can only see if we find shelter and give ourselves enough distance.

As we live our lives, if we are observant, we can try to catch the underlying waves of life very early on. We can let the water slowly and gracefully bring us along.

If we are still early enough and observant enough, we can catch the tide and let the long waves carry us. They can carry us to where we want to go with only minor corrections.

If we just react to the immediate waves, we get buffeted and caught in the breakers. We get caught in the immediate riptide;

we become caught and pulled under. If we reach our destinations, it is only with significant effort.

By having enough distance, we can recognize the longer and underlying wave patterns and use them to assist us in getting to our destinations. In the words of Albert Schweitzer, "Just as the wave cannot exist for itself, but is ever a part of the heaving surface of the ocean, so must I never live my life for itself, but always in the experience which is going on around me."

CHAPTER 11

The Lights

In the right light, at the right time, everything is extraordinary.

—Aaron Rose

*A*nother way to think of the differences that correspond to the limbs, trees, and habitats is in the context of light. We are surrounded by all sorts of light, each of which impacts us in a different fashion. I also think of entanglement as strobe light thoughts, sunrise thoughts, and universe thoughts.

Strobe light thoughts are those short bursts of ideas which demand immediate attention but do not last. If you have ever been in a dark room when a strobe light starts to flash, you know that you are constantly reacting to the flash of bright light. You don't have a chance to adjust as the moments of darkness are briefly broken by an overwhelming light. You never get a chance to adjust. You never get a chance to focus. You never get a chance to think.

Sunset thoughts are those graceful, slow-paced thoughts that take time to fully develop. If you have ever watched the sky as the sun slowly sets, the colors of the sky go from a light blue to shades of purple and pink and then magically transform into a dark, inky black. You see a graceful, slow, deliberate, enriching movement.

In the background of the universe is a beautiful, mysterious glow of infrared light. Seen across entire sky the glow is the light from the stars that linger between the galaxies. Like the infrared light, there are "universe thoughts." Universe thoughts are those thoughts that are quietly, steadily, always there. They are always present, even if we don't think that we see or hear them. This is a perpetual light. This is a glow that your eyes will have to adjust to rather than a light with so many lumens that you could read a book by.

All are necessary in their own ways, although the first one is ephemeral, and the others have lasting value.

By placing equal importance on the immediate waves and strobe light entanglements, we become overwhelmed with all of the entanglements. We realize that when we find distance, we can see the sweep of our narratives as we lay bare our hearts and minds. We can begin to see how entanglements surrounding us emerge.

CHAPTER 12

Emergence

Man is equally incapable of seeing the nothingness from which he emerges and the infinity in which he is engulfed.

—Blaise Pascal

*L*ike the mountains and gorges that emerged around us, it appears that out of all of the entanglements and waves, something is emerging.

We have seen the tensions and the struggles surrounding the emergence of an industrial society from an agrarian culture and then from an industrial to information culture. We have seen the difficulties with the emergence of the age of enlightenment from what has been called a spiritual era. We have seen the difficulties in the convergence of Western (Homeric) and Eastern (Indian) worldviews.

Jeffrey Goldstein provided an appropriate definition of emergence in the journal *Emergence*. He defined emergence as "the arising of novel and coherent structures, patterns and properties during the process of self-organization in complex systems."

According to Samuel Alexander, emergence is not merely neutral. Rather, emergence is something new; emergence is a fresh creation. The process is a "distinctive quality." This quality is not resultant, it is active.

I am one of very many who believe that our current period is part of the emergence of a third axial age. An axial age is a period in which the traditional relationships between religion, secularity, and traditional thought are changing. As noted by Jacques Barzun and others the last half millennium has seen great transitions throughout the Western world. Each has brought extreme change. An example that Barzun uses is the remaking of the commercial and social worlds shaped by the rise of Protestantism and by the decline of hereditary monarchies.

As we examine and reflect upon political, religious, and social trails, it appears as if we are moving into a new axial age. Karl Jaspers initially used the phrase axial age to describe a period in which "the spiritual foundations of humanity were laid simultaneously and independently" by thinkers such as Plato, the Buddha, and Confucius. Karen Armstrong used the term in her books *The Great Transformation* and *A History of God* to argue that the Enlightenment was a "second axial age."

Emergence only happens through either cultivation or erosion. Do we cultivate the changes, or do we simply get caught in erosion? How do we choose? What do we choose? Do we float along on the steady tide, the long waves, or do we get caught in the riptide of the short waves?

Other times and places have thought the same. I am not so naive as to believe that this is the culmination of history. In the words of David Rothkopf, I want to avoid "the kind of temporal narcissism from which we all filter: the desire to view the period in which we live as a unique moment in history, above and apart from all that have come before."

This is a unique moment, but each moment is a unique moment. Each moment is part of this continuous emergence. How do we find the distance to cultivate the emergence of beauty and love?

CHAPTER 13

The Clutter

At every moment there is in us an infinity of perceptions.

—Gottfried Wilhelm Leibniz

*I*n the mornings, we heard a multitude of birds signing. Our morning alarm clock was the calls that they made. Each bird had its own unique song; each bird was beautiful in and of itself. While complex in their variety, we could barely distinguish one from another. Each bird struggled to be heard over the others.

The complexity surrounding our entanglements leads to a mental clutter that can be as difficult to sort through as the birdsongs. Entanglement clutter is one of the most complex challenges confronting us, and sorting through the entanglements is one of our greatest struggles. Like a gathering that has gone out of control and ending up as a mess of hundreds of strangers, our number and types of entanglements in this hyperentangled world have grown to an overwhelming, incomprehensible number.

We can think of the clutter in the context of a conversation. In this context, there is a conundrum. If you are listening to one person, you can give that person your full attention. If two people are talking at the same time, you can usually pick out one of the two voices, listen to it, and understand it.

When three people are talking simultaneously, you can still only pick out one voice. You have to pick out the one voice that you will listen to. It should not be the loudest voice. It should not be the harshest voice. It should just be quietly the most important voice.

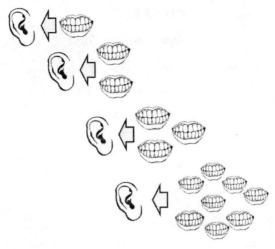

Chatter

Each voice is part of the background and causes entanglement at some level. Leibniz expressed a philosophy rooted in the idea that within each substance there is an expression of the entire universe. However, he also saw through his account of "petites perceptions" or "minute perceptions" that many things distract and entangle us. As he fully said in his preface to *The New Essays on Human Understanding*, "At every moment there is in us an infinity of perceptions, unaccompanied by awareness or reflection; that is, of alterations in the soul itself, of which we are unaware because these impressions are either too minute and too numerous, or else too unvarying, so that they are not sufficiently distinctive on their own."

When conversations increase by multiples of volume, variety, and velocity, there is no way that your brain can even pick out one voice. It all turns into white noise. You have to find a way to pick out which wave you will "listen" to.

You have to find a way to shelter yourself from the immediate waves. To find shelter, you need to cultivate contemplation.

CHAPTER 14

Shelter from the Rain

Life isn't finding shelter in the storm.
It is about learning to dance in the rain.

—Sherrily Kenyon

We have all had occasions when the soft drops of rain wake us up. Rain has a soft sound that relaxes us. There is a type of rain which quietly hits the windows and gently calls us from slumber. There is a gentle rain that waters the crops and the lawns.

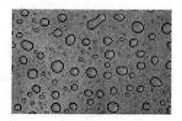

Raindrop patterns

But not all rain is gentle. Taiwan's climate is a tropical one with an annual monsoon season. It has those pounding rains that characterize so much of Asia.

Monsoons are the sheets of water which overwhelm everything, which wash everything in their path away. Monsoons are the unrelenting, brutal rains that seem to never stop.

Entanglements into today's world resemble monsoons: relentless, pounding, violent, overwhelming, and immediate. I would posit that our entanglements center around three pounding vectors that resemble monsoon rains: volume, variety, and velocity.

Volume

As I wrote this, the number of global mobile connections—entanglements—surpassed five billion, within a total population of seven billion. Eighteen months earlier, the number of connections had been four billion. In the next twelve months, it is predicted there will be over six billion global entanglements. The global penetration rate of devices connected to the Internet has moved from 60 percent at four billion to 74 percent at the five billion mark. There are regions in the world where individuals have multiple mobility devices, leading to rather unique position of having a penetration rate that exceeds 100 percent. Internet radio and television have given birth to hundreds of thousands of unique channels. Marketing is microtargeted to particular individuals. The numbers are almost overwhelming.

Variety

We don't become entangled by just one time and in just one way. With globalization and social networks, opportunities to connect are ever increasing. Every click, every call, every viral video, every trip, every product, each is a new potential entanglement. Each causes a different reaction, and offers us a way to embrace the entanglement.

Velocity

For the purposes of this conversation, I differentiate between speed and velocity. Using a common definition, while speed describes only how fast an object is moving, velocity is speed in a given direction. Velocity encompasses both the speed and the direction of the object's motion. In our hyperentangled world, the relative velocity is ever increasing. The speed of entanglements has increased. The direction that entanglements could come in from and depart to has also dramatically increased. It is no longer a world of slow speeds and single direction. It is a hyperspeed, multidimensional world.

All three vectors have increased exponentially. Traditionally, entanglements were physical and local. We normally acted within our tribes, our villages, our own small geographic regions. This has changed, as evidenced by the virtualization, globalization, and hyperentanglements surrounding us.

The question is, what can let us learn to dance in the rain? What will let us appreciate the rain rather than simply getting wet? What will let us appreciate love and beauty rather than simply existing within the immediate waves?

CHAPTER 15

Contemplation

A rock pile ceases to be a rock pile the moment a single man contemplates it, bearing within him the image of a cathedral.

—Antoine de Saint-Exupéry

*A*s we walked along, we encountered clearings that let us see a greater perspective. We found the places that sheltered us from the rain.

As the week progressed, we learned how to adjust our pace in order to allow us to see more of the clearings, to find the places that allowed us to see differently. We were able to see not just the limbs but also trees. More importantly, we were able to find the distance to see the habitat. Critically, we were able to see them as part of a continuum.

Our measured pace allowed us to become aware of ourselves and to become aware of our surroundings. As we unplugged from our daily sensory overload, we regained our sense of self. We were able to use the silence, stillness, and solitude of the hike to recognize and cultivate the transition from seeing simply the branches to seeing the great whole.

We found that our transformation was not a passive and quiet process. Inertia did not bring us along. Our transformation required active cultivation and deep engagement; it required contemplation. We were not sitting around with vacant stares. We were actively engaged in our journey.

Contemplation gives us the ability to find shelter from the rain. Contemplation is a journey toward deep self-discovery.

We find that contemplation had to be done within the context of an active life. Following Saint Augustine's third way, we find that contemplation could not only be done in daily, it needed to be done in daily life. To be fully realized, contemplation had to be done in daily life.

Through Saint Teresa, Saint John, and others, Western thinkers saw that we could experience contemplation daily. We are still beginning to rediscover this lost stream of our spiritual heritage. Eastern thinkers in the Buddhist, Hindu, Taoist, and Confucian streams marvel that we did not see this as self-evident from the onset.

I don't presume to offer a set series of steps to a life of mystical fulfillment. This discussion is simply a recognition and acknowledgment that fosters and enables a life that fully integrates and respects contemplation as an essential element.

I don't ever presume to contend that everyone is a mystic. Contemplative nature is universal. Mysticism is not.

The attributes of contemplative nature are universal. Further, these attributes can be cultivated.

I also do not presume to offer a concrete series of steps. Our journeys all differ.

I do contend that there is an absurdity in trying to live without contemplation.

CHAPTER 16

Contemplation Framed

*I live not in dreams, but in contemplation of a reality
that is perhaps the future.*

—Rainer Maria Rilke

*L*ife is framed by perceptions, by experiences, and by numerous other factors. We instinctively establish frameworks in order to better understand our lives. Through contemplation, we have an opportunity to reframe with a sense of awareness.

I have found it useful to try to frame contemplation. As merely a reference model, I have broken it down into five foundational elements and three pillars. The foundational elements are conceptual, continuous, connective, creative, and contextual. This foundation supports the pillars of contemplation, which are silence, stillness and solitude. I am going to briefly summarize the foundational elements.

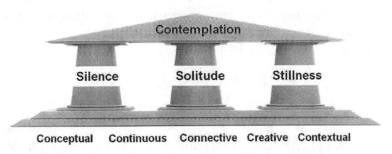

Contemplation framed

Conceptual

As a conceptual process, contemplation is an activity concerned with the relationships of ideas. It is a calm and intentional consideration, examination, and evaluation of self and of society. Contemplation can take the form of structured exercises that allow you to make entanglements and gain insights, or it can be simply the ability to allow insights to occur. The goal throughout is to allow yourself to see the larger context and establish pathways that may not have been there before.

Continuous

Contemplation is a conscious, continuous process. As a continuous process, contemplation is an ongoing activity. It is not an activity done in a vacuum. Rather, it is an integrated activity within our daily lives. It cannot be done as a stand-alone activity. It cannot be done in isolation.

Connective

As a connective process, contemplation is an activity linked with and dependent upon other activities. We all have a yearning to relate to others and to have them like what we do. We always feel better when other validate us. There is no way to disassociate contemplation from the entanglements or our innate desire to connect with others. Again, contemplation is not done in isolation.

Creative

In the process of contemplation, we create a space to allow ourselves to unfold and be creative. We develop the ability to connect our exterior and our interior selves. Besides being nomadic, I think that we are fundamentally creative beings.

We have an innate desire to bring something new into the world. Contemplation lets us draw upon the rich streams around us in order to fully engage in the world and draw upon our experiences in order to allow intentional communities to flourish and awaken beauty. It is an activity where something new is produced.

Contextual

As a contextual process, contemplation is an activity within a specific situation, time, and place. We can take our own experiences and examine them in greater depth and in relationship to our environments and beliefs. Our understanding of the contemplative context is not just our stepping away but achieving a perspective of our world. Contemplation is an activity within a specific situation.

Using these elements to help understand the foundational aspects of contemplation, we can now explore the nuances of the three pillars of contemplation: silence, stillness and solitude.

CHAPTER 17

Silence

In every moment of time, man through silence can be with the origins of all things.

—Max Picard

We spent many hours hiking through places where quiet filled our ears. Growing up in a slightly rural area, I love how silence can surround and embrace me. I recognize psychologically how much I depend upon it.

Our hike started in a major city full of the routine noises. We had cars, trucks, and buses moving around us; all of these caused a din that surrounded us at all times. It had the crush of people, the chatter of the streets, and the blare of the outdoor advertisements.

As we went around more bends and moved farther and farther away from the urban environment each day, the days and nights became much quieter. There were fewer people and less traffic. There was less congestion and chatter. We became more removed from the electronic connectedness that surrounds all of us. Without all of the electronic devices that cause a constant numbing audio bombardment of our lives, we had to embrace silence.

We have white noise surrounding us almost all of the time. We have the sounds of the city or the sounds of the country providing a backdrop to our lives. How often do we make an opportunity to embrace total silence? Or do we allow ourselves to be constantly distracted by the ticking of a clock in the background, the hum of the computer, the "bing" of an e-mail, or the siren's call of an instant message?

How do we create a space that allows us not to just filter the noises out but to remove the noise? Filtering is not a complete removal of the noise. It does not eliminate; the filters merely mask. The conditions that cause noise to occur remain. To fully engage in life we need the distance found in silence.

The Swiss philosopher Max Picard (1888–1965) was one of Thomas Merton's sources of inspiration. In *The World of Silence*, Picard wrote of the nature of silence. He contended that silence lies as the mostly unrecognized source of our own beings. Picard put forward the proposition that silence can transform and awaken us.

As Picard noted, silence is always present, even if it is not recognized and acknowledged. Silence gives breadth and depth to a conversation by creating distance. Words do not exist within the narrow space occupied by the two speakers. Rather, words exist and come from the place where silence is listening; it is what gives the speakers distance.

Heidegger, Picard, and others maintained that speech frequently regresses to the lowest possible denominator. Speech degenerates into chatter. We see this in the chatter of the social networks and our entanglements.

Chatter overwhelms us. It overwhelms us by its immediacy and causes us to forget the value of silence.

Chatter imprisons us in a cell of immediacy. It is a cell from which we are unable to wholly free ourselves unless we can place silence in our lives.

Sadly, we are not even aware of our current loss of silence. The space formerly occupied by the silence has become so full of chatter and strobe light thoughts that nothing appears to be missing.

In the space where formerly silence could let an idea could slowly bloom, the erosive nature of the immediate waves of entanglements can instantaneously bury a new creation. Without distance and cultivation, silence has no hope. Silence gives us the distance between the waves to allow our thoughts to lengthen.

Our social network and media-filled age cause new and special challenges. The volume, variety, and velocity of chatter surrounding us have dramatically increased. It induces a false sense of security. We imagine—and it is an illusion—that the chatter and immediate entanglements represent something more sustainable. Without the substance of silence, we become oppressed by the many entanglements that crowd us in every move of our lives.

When we live in the noise, we are impacted by it. In the end, the noise around us not only is something made by us, the noise also makes us. In the words of Picard, "When we are silent, we find ourselves."

As with the gorges surrounding us, when transformations happen too quickly, the landscape simply erodes away. The underlying soil and underlying beauty are pushed into the nearest river to wash away into the ocean. The underlying waves found through silence, stillness, and solitude allow for lasting beauty to develop.

CHAPTER 18

Stillness

Wisdom comes with the ability to be still.
Just look and listen. No more is needed.

—Eckhart Tolle

As we began our cross-island journey, we got caught in the invariable traffic tie-ups and construction projects. They caused us to journey at a significantly slower speed than we had intended. We wanted to get where we were going. We wanted to get there now.

However, as we ride along highways, at high speeds and with the traffic moving freely, we miss a lot. The speed, the other cars, the sound barriers alongside the road, and many things encourage us to miss the details. In order to see deeply, we need to see with stillness. In order to feel deeply, we need to feel with stillness.

Stillness understimulates all of our senses, which is why it necessary. Stillness slows us so we see details. Stillness slows us down so we can see the nuances. Stillness slows us down so we can see the depth of the world around us.

Stillness is a gift. It is a gift that we can readily give ourselves. It is a gift that helps reduce the moments of anxiety by giving us distance. It is a gift that lets us see beyond the immediate to the underlying. Stillness slows us down so we can engage the world rather than being entertained by it.

Sadly, stillness is taught as a punishment rather than a gift. We send children to "time-out." We yell at them to settle down. The imposed moments of stillness become weighted down with negative baggage.

Stillness is not found within the caricature of a monk or yogi locked in an upright position for hours. Rather, stillness is an intentional act that calms you down. You stop and pause. You stop and don't fidget. You stop and cast yourself into deeper waters.

Stillness lets you enter into that place where nothing and no one can distract you. Stillness allows for the purposeful emergence of love and the perennial.

The immediate waves create an ADHD culture that encourages to us to be so busy doing that we never get to the point of finishing. We can create a culture that doesn't value busyness. We can define our weeks not by checking off things that we do but rather what we accomplish.

Stillness doesn't just happen. Stillness needs to be cultivated. We react to our environments when we let the immediate waves push us along.

Like silence, stillness is foundational and always present. It is part of the foundation of life itself. With silence, stillness, and solitude, we allow ourselves to find what really matters.

CHAPTER 19

Solitude

Solitude shows us what should be;
society shows us what we are.

—Robert Cecil

*H*ave you ever come across a house nestled all alone? Or have you ever seen a cottage so remote that it could be a scene from a fable or fairy tale?

In this territory traditionally reserved for Taiwanese aboriginals, we infrequently came across small cottages—cottages inhabited by individuals who had chosen to separate themselves from the rest of society. These are people who have chosen to be solitary. While bearded hermits living alone in the desert or Thoreau on the shore of Walden Pond are the images normally evoked by the word solitude, I can see the faces of the solitary in everyday life. People who are comfortable within themselves.

In the words of Picard, there is a fundamental "need for silence and solitude in order to allow a person to develop an inviolable personal integrity." There is an "essential and unique" place that we can truly connect, but a place can only be reached through the cultivated contemplation based in solitude, stillness, and silence.

The fundamental of solitude is being alone. It is not being an individualist. It is not being isolated. It is not being lonely. It is not being without any contact, the image of a bearded desert dweller notwithstanding.

Solitude, within an active, contemplative life, follows the premise found in Pascal's *Note*. Everyone is a solitary in the existential sense.

Solitude means being able to find the space to think by yourself. Solitude means finding yourself. Solitude means finding your own trail among the entanglements.

Aristotle considered it important that we maintain distance, distance between and among ourselves and others, ourselves and events, ourselves and art. Contemplation and solitude allows us to develop our sense of catharsis and gives us the room to address life.

In a chatter-filled life, the constant bombardment of other people's thoughts submerges you. This submergence creates a cacophony in which it is impossible to hear any voice, much less your own. This submergence marinates you in conventional wisdom. Solitude lets you intentionally shelter yourself from the bombardment. Solitude allows you to swim out of the path of the immediate waves.

Merton stressed the distinction between the solitary and individualist. The individualist does not seek contemplation; the individualist seeks a heightened self-consciousness, essentially a form of narcissism. The solitary seeks something. The solitary seeks the underlying.

Solitude is all the more necessary today when the entanglements swallow us up into the faceless mass described by Arendt. We succumb to the temptation to immerse ourselves in the mass of other men.

To paraphrase Arendt, we don't escape to the mountains or the desert. We escape into the crowd. We escape into a formless sea of irresponsibility. There is no more dangerous solitude than that of the man who is lost in a crowd because he does not know he is alone.

We will never be fully conscious of the beauty of solitude if we allow society to fill our minds and hearts with diversions and distractions. Solitude does not isolate you or cut you off from contemporary problems. In the spirit of catharsis, solitude allows you to find the distance to think about them more deeply.

CHAPTER 20

Cultivation

Only he is free who cultivates his own thoughts,
and strives without fear to do justice to them

—Berthold Auerbach

*A*s we hiked, we passed by hectare after hectare, acre after acre of tea bushes. We crossed through some of the best-known tea-growing regions in the world. Outrageously expensive and beautifully delicate, these leaves were the result of centuries of cultivation. While tea can be found in nature, the leaves are more precious, flavorful and nuanced when properly cultivated.

Tea cultivation

Our lives are also like that. Our lives are more precious, flavorful and nuanced when properly cultivated. We can select, gather, seed, farm, and harvest our lives. We can cultivate our own visions and own experiences.

As with tea leaves, our doxa and our ability to contemplate can be cultivated. Our experiences can be intentionally cultivated for ourselves, for others, and for our communities. These experiences become foundational to our doxa.

Doxa is the stuff that "goes without saying." It is the theory that we instinctively absorb from our native culture what we need to make sense of the world. Doxa is the series of assumptions, presumptions, and "common sense" ideas we have about our world and how it works. Our absorption is an inescapable cultural process.

Doxa is both a medium that creates and simultaneously a rulebook by which we figure it all out. In the general theory of doxastic practices, we have constellations of belief-forming mechanisms, interwoven with other practices and projects of ours, which have "stood the test of time" and produce mostly consistent sets of beliefs.

There is a simultaneous expression and teaching of doxa; it is a self-reinforcing cycle. It is not an abstract theory. Doxa is the name for the really mundane and routinely overlooked daily backdrop of our lives. Routinely invisible and seamless, it often goes unchallenged.

Our genes are completely entangled with our doxa. It has become clear to scientists that our brains and our actions are interwoven. As actions transform our brains, our brains transform our actions. In this circumstance, the "nature versus nurture" debate is simply ridiculous. We ought to focus on what happens given the context of our experiences.

Our experiences become the seedlings of our life; our experiences become the moments of insight. We are formed by habits that we cultivate. We can define by our experiences. If we choose, our world can be an experience rich, beauty filled environment.

Without contemplation of these experiences, we are shortchanged. In our hyperconnected world, we have become overwhelmed by the variety, velocity and volume experiences. By focusing on the immediate waves, we shortchange ourselves on the necessary but time-consuming process of forming the associative networks needed to fully engage in the world. By not finding distance, we shortchange ourselves from organizing experience meaningfully.

You can cultivate love. You can cultivate fear. You can cultivate short waves. You can cultivate long waves. You can choose.

In a world that values the immediate, we need the actual experience itself. We cannot cultivate with only an analysis or an executive summary.

Cultivation is the process by which we contemplatively choose.

CHAPTER 21

Erosion

Erosion is a slow and insidious process.

—David Pimentel

As we walked, we saw that the landscape was just not the result of cultivation. The landscape was also the result of tens of thousands of years of natural erosion. This erosion was not chosen.

Erosion is both a gradual and a rapid wearing away of something. Erosion is a natural process. The earth's surface is worn down by natural forces like running water, wind, glaciers, and waves. It breaks down rocks, mountains, and land surfaces. In turn, these broken pieces are carried away by wind, rain, or rushing rivers.

As commonly defined, the rate of erosion depends on many factors. These factors include the amount and intensity of precipitation, the average temperature, as well as the typical temperature range, seasonality, wind speed, and storm frequency. If you alter even slightly any one of these factors, something different emerges. Wide temperature variations cause one pattern; heavy rainstorms cause a different pattern.

This natural erosion can create great things of beauty, from the river erosion at the heart of the American Grand Canyon, to the coastal erosion of the Orkney Islands, or the glacial erosion of the Swiss Matterhorn, or the wind erosion of the Navajo desert, this process can cause landforms to develop and can shape wondrous natural features.

More often, we saw evidence of a different type of erosion around us, around the fields, around the roads, around the bridges, and around the mountains. This is what I would categorize as induced erosion.

Induced erosion is the erosion caused by human land-use policies that have a secondary or tertiary order of effect. From agricultural runoff that results in the silting of estuaries and runoff from the roads that pollute the bays, our choices can induce unintended erosion.

The tea orchards we went through were a typical feature of the region. They covered large parts of the hillslopes. In some cases, the hillslopes were badly degraded due to the erosive nature of the crops cultivated on them. Even as the farmers cultivated them, tea orchards and land could still be in bad shape.

Erosion happens in every aspect of our lives. We have to both recognize and be mindful of the erosion's effects. We can use contemplation to give us the distance to recognize the effects of erosion and ensure that we don't act blindly.

Things do not usually normally occur in a single, massive slide but are generally the result of small, gradual slides. These small, gradual slides result in the hillside being swept away.

Our challenge is to recognize that one seemingly innocuous step leads to another, which leads to another—until the new behaviors, which were originally only slight deviations, become our new normal, our new doxa, and we proceed as if nothing is wrong.

Cultivation and erosion are both part of the emergence process. Each has its place. Along this trail, we saw evidence of both cultivation and erosion. We saw the result of tangible actions that helped create something.

On our own journeys, we can read the guides. We can glance through the online photos. We can read the travel reviews. But we need to actually take the first step in order to begin our journeys.

To use the phrases that are fraught with connotations, we need to put one foot in front of the other to start down the trail, and we can think about thinking. However, how do we act about thinking? What actions can we take to cultivate contemplation? What are some of the metaphors we can use to cultivate contemplation in our daily lives?

CHAPTER 22

Seeing That It Is Not So Simple

Everything should be made as simple as possible,
but not simpler.

—Albert Einstein

*H*ow many times have you heard one of the following?

Make it simple

Boil it down

Top five bullets

One of the first actions that we can take to cultivate contemplation is to embrace the idea that the world is not simple. How much can you summarize something and still allow it to have any meaning? For a moment, set aside the lack of substance and the lack of rigour of the chatter you commonly hear and consider how long it takes for someone to say it.

As already noted, with the volume, variety, and velocity of entanglements, we see a constant increase in complexity and a continual crush of inputs. This increase in entanglements causes our world to become much more complex. The industrial world was more complex than the agrarian world. The information world is much more complex than the industrial world. Many times, do we cope by only simplifying this complexity?

Contemplation allows us to accept and understand that things are not so simple. Without recognizing and acknowledging the underlying complexity of our world, our actions result in a depth of thought that is Twitter deep. Our ideas become expressed in nine-second bursts, which is the average length of a sound bite in broadcast news stories or the amount it takes to speak the 140 characters in a tweet. Our mental mirrors only become illuminated by strobe light thoughts.

By choosing a few words that convey the strongest possible meanings in nine seconds or less, we embrace the superficial rather than the real. By using phrases that try to win the argument without taking the time for argument, we cheapen the discourse.

An example of this process of reduction of depth and corresponding loss of nuance is with the recording industry. We have a great scale for musical fidelity from live, vinyl hi-fi, CD/MP3/iTunes, to ringtones. Audio manufactures used the term *high fidelity* as a way to describe the faithful sound reproduction

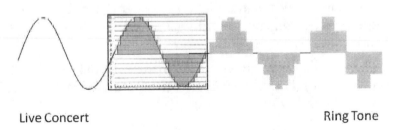

Live Concert   Ring Tone

Bit sampling and block sizes

In the digitalization process, we process information in blocks, with a block representing the number of audio samples which will be used before giving output.

Sampling does not always work. The fewer the samples, the easier it is for the computer or our minds to process. A larger number of samples will give a great correlation to the actual sound wave. But the large sampling takes significantly more computer processing power and time. However, the output is closer to the true sound.

Living near Washington DC, I am fortunate to be continually exposed to live music in intimate spaces. There is nothing as magical as having a soprano or a classical violinist performing mere feet away from you. You get to experience the full range of emotions. You get to experience the flaws. You get to experience the nuances. You get to experience humanity. Experiences cannot be reduced or simplified.

As we listen to MP3s or CDs, they sound "flat." The digital medium gives us only a semblance of the live; it is an illusion. As with our sound-bite society or uncontemplative world, we have become so taken with the advantages of the digital that we fail to recognize its limitations. A digital file is merely a shadow of the memory; the memory is a mere shadow of the actual experience.

At the end of the day, we have the same internal problem. We are analog and not digital. We don't live our lives by chunking experiences into distinct blocks. We live our lives on a continuum.

Our task, our trick will be to learn how to deliver higher fidelity in our lives when we've spent so much effort squeezing the life out of life in the first place.

CHAPTER 23

Not Bypassing

Character is that which reveals moral purpose,
exposing the class of things a man chooses and avoids.

—Aristotle

*E*ach day, we learned new skills. When we tried them out, we realized that we had to, at least initially, follow the instructions step by step. Much like when artists find a new song, they practice it, they perfect it, and then they adapt it to make it their own.

The second action we can take is not to contemplatively bypass. We grow by going through the entire process of finding, practicing, perfecting, and then adapting. We don't grow by simply jumping to the conclusion.

There is a fallacy that we can go directly to the end and realize all of the benefits. We need to go through the entire process in order to fully understand and internalize the changes.

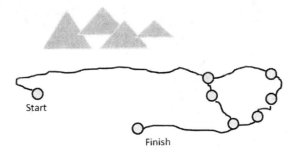

A trail with a bypass

Contemplative bypass occurs when we seek to avoid genuine contact with our entanglements. It occurs when we attempt to get to the "end" without taking the full journey. It occurs when we ignore our need to work at the cognitive, physical, emotional, and interpersonal levels.

The trail shown above has possible bypass. We could take that bypass in order to get to the finish faster. However, in doing so, we may miss a waterfall, a rushing river, or some other point that would give great depth to the journey.

Contemplative bypass jeopardizes our long-term development because it renders our development incomplete. Without the integration and internalization that occurs when we fully go through the thought process, our development and lives are stunted.

CHAPTER 24

Recognizing the Impact

In everyone's life, at some time, our inner fire goes out. It is then burst into flame by an encounter with another human being. We should all be thankful for those people who rekindle the inner spirit.

—Albert Schweitzer

One of the thrills of traveling to a new place is that you get to directly encounter something new every day. This hike was no different. Each day, we encountered something new.

From a new mist-laden mountain pass, to a steep ravine, to a treacherous bridge, we were experiencing something novel at every turn. Each day, we encountered something new. It could be sights, sounds, or smells. We experience something new every day of our lives.

But so what? Who cares? What do these encounters actually mean? In this hyperentangled world, how can we determine the impact and meaning of the particular entanglement? Do we just treat them all equally? Are they all simply wisps of dust that drift by, with no real substance or meaning? We need to appropriately recognize and acknowledge the impact of our entanglements.

We can all think of instances and specific times in life that in hindsight were decisive on whom we've become. We can recall encounters that shifted our lives. We can also recall encounters that did not impact us but dramatically altered the course of someone else's journey. There are times in life when we reach critical points and make crucial decisions, points and decisions that we are not aware of until after that particular time has passed.

Recalling the conversation analogy, we have seen that we need to find approaches to understand the multiple occasions of entanglement that impact us. In principle, we could try to understand each entanglement. But trying to understand each entanglement is not only cumbersome but unenlightening.

Each conversation does not have the same weight. Each entanglement does not have the same weight; the weight for one actor may be very different than the weight for another. Contemplation lets us understand the weights.

I contend that the impact of our entanglements is a combination of variables: novelty, frequency, intensity, and speed.

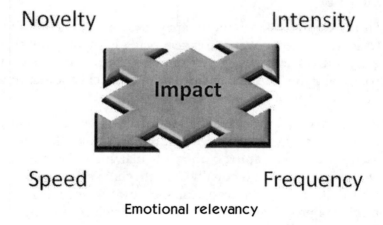

Emotional relevancy

Novelty

As a resident of Washington DC region, I get to experience the yearly influx of tourists. While it would be easy to complain about the additional people, the lack of knowledge of the traffic patterns, and a large list of other things, I think that it is much more interesting to see their reactions as they first see the places that were previously only seen on a screen. The wonder and excitement of the visitors finally experiencing firsthand things that were previously only flickering images is delightful.

We want novelty. We crave novelty. We remember our first times: our first kisses, our first loves, our first experiences of something. The newness and uniqueness causes us to fundamentally shift our perspectives. We see this with children as they explore the new world that always surrounds them. We see this with travelers as they experience new cultures and cuisines. We see this in the encounters that relight our inner fires. Our brains are hardwired for it, and in turn, we naturally respond to it.

By way of a summary to ground the discussion, there is a chemical component to this. Novelty triggers excitement and surprise, which in turn stimulates the production of dopamine. While dopamine has many functions, I'm focused on the fact that dopamine neurons are chemical encoders which signal teaching behaviours as they trigger a chemical reward for a particular action. In short, dopamine reinforces something because of the pleasure it triggers.

With five hundred, one thousand, fifteen hundred Facebook "friends," we have become enthralled with the novelty of "connecting" that we forget why we connect. Like a caffeine addict who starts to suffer from caffeine poisoning, there is a point at which novelty and the dopamine become too much. It creates an overload. The overload poisons your system, shutting it down until only the immediate waves are the ones we can see. We need to find the right balance, and we find that balance through contemplation.

Frequency

With repetition, experiences become part of your life's background. On this trail, I remember working with one of the Scouts on his knot-tying skills. The young man's face was scrunched in puzzlement as we started the process of how to tie a certain knot again. We had already done it numerous times, and we were about to start again.

I could relate. Knot tying has never been a strength of mine. We kept practicing over and over until we got it right. We saw that frequency mattered.

In the words of Matthew Kelly, "Our lives changes when our habits change." Experiences and emotions done or felt over and over again become foundational to your life. As when a musician wants to perform a specific piece of music, we have to find it, we have to practice it, and we have to make it our own.

If our actions get reinforced early on, if we repeat them, if we cultivate them, they become self-sustaining. Actions form the basis for all our habits and beliefs, from the simplest thing all the way up to complex ideologies.

How many times do you need to make a knot in order for it to become part of you? What actions do we choose in order to make something our own?

Intensity

Intensity is a complex word. It connotes passion, force, pigment, shades, units of measurement, and commitment. In the context of understanding entanglements, I mean to use it in all of these aspects.

I use intensity as a way to describe entanglements, which is not a new idea. Research is beginning to reveal that those with high- and low-intensity levels think about and react to events very differently. Individuals who have a deep emotional intensity and a better understanding of those entanglements have a more complex sense of themselves and lead lives that are more engaged than do those whose entanglements are less strong. Further, I would contend that we can cultivate intensity and learn how to think deeply.

Speed

Recall that I am differentiating between speed and velocity. Our ability to recognize impact is not a velocity issue. It is a speed issue. Speed in this context is the way in which entanglements resonate. Do the entanglements resonate slowly and deeply, or do they resonate quickly and reinforce existing pathways?

Studies show that we are dual-process thinkers. We have a slow, deliberate thinking style and a rapid, automatic style; both systems are concurrently running. The slow, deliberate style is a conscious, reasoning one. The rapid style is an unconscious, intuitive one.

Fast entanglements strengthen existing neural entanglements, while the slower changes create new neural entanglements. Lasting changes occur when we pay close attention and conduct ourselves with close attention and use both styles to see the underlying and to reinforce of our understanding of it.

External forces and internal pressures restructure our "wiring" and restructure it in relatively short order. In the words of J. Z. Young, "Every action leaves some permanent print upon the nervous tissue."

Both are necessary. Both have their appropriate places.

One of the skills we taught the Scouts was how to properly start fires. To have a fire, you need to have three key elements: fuel, oxygen, and a catalyst. The problem that younger Scouts generally have is that they forget the importance of having all three elements working together properly.

In our own lives, all four of the variables—novelty, frequency, intensity, and speed—are necessary to start our own fires. Once we acknowledge and understand the four variables, we can choose the way we recognize and acknowledge our entanglements, cultivate contemplation, and engage life.

CHAPTER 25

Finding Distance

We may go to the moon, but that's not very far. The greatest distance we have to cover still lies within us.

—Charles de Gaulle

*I*n the mornings, we stood in the mist and felt as if these were timeless places. As the mists cleared, we looked around and looked at the maps to see where we were headed that day.

We couldn't see all of the switchbacks and gorges. The distance on the map did not reflect the distance we would experience. Both space and time were expanded and compressed, a compression and expansion which makes our world concurrently aspatial and atemporal.

As with the theorists who believe that space may be an illusion, we came to realize that distance is frequently a mirage. We didn't initially realize that while a crow could fly rather quickly, our trail would meander. This was part of the aspatial nature to our journey. Our lives do not follow a set, straight trail. Our lives meander.

Our path determines the distance we travel. One of the paths between two points may be the shortest; one may be longish. We may even return "home" essentially having no change in position. Nevertheless, we would have traveled. This is also part of the aspatial nature of our lives. Our position may not have changed. But the distance we would have traveled would not be zero.

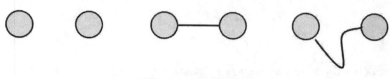

What is distance?

There is distance. A distance we need to recognize. Our recognition of distance is crucial. Aristotle considered it important that we maintain distance—distance between and among ourselves and others, ourselves and events, ourselves and art.

For Aristotle, distance allows us to develop a sense of catharsis. Catharsis is an "emotional cleansing." Catharsis purifies us and gives us the room to address life.

Distancing is a coping strategy that is usually learned early in life. Routinely automatic, it is a way for us to cope when we become overwhelmed with the demands around us. While each of us has a threshold for what we can tolerate, we each do have a threshold.

Self-distancing is the ability to become an engaged observer rather than a participant. From that distanced perspective, you have the ability to understand your feelings. The key is not to get immersed in your own emotions and to cultivate a more detached view.

Catharsis demands that we create a sense of distance. Contemplation takes the next step. Contemplation lets us see that distance. Distance may not be the straight line simply joining initial and final positions. Our start and stop positions are merely arbitrary points.

Contemplative distancing is finding the appropriate selection of distance between oneself and the entanglement throughout an encounter. You need to cultivate the ability to separate yourself enough to find perspective. Distancing is an intrinsic result of the contemplative process.

In the words of Pope Benedict, "The contemplation of Christ in our life does not distance us from reality. It makes us even more involved in human affairs, because the Lord, drawing us to Himself in prayer, enables us to remain close to all our brothers and sisters in His love." Our contemplation of life also draws us closer to reality.

Contemplation allows us to intentionally find distance amid the vectors of entanglement.

CHAPTER 26

Exploring Betweenness

The web of betweenness is still there but in order to become a presence again, it needs to be invoked.

—John O'Donohue

*W*e began in a city and then moved through farmland. Eventually, we transitioned into wilderness and ended our journey in a different urban setting.

Betweenness marked the transition from one to another of these environments. Betweenness marked the moments of transitions; betweenness marked transition zones where two dissimilar things mix.

Our mental zoning maps should recognize transition zones; the zones that provide a buffer between incompatible mental land uses. These transition zones allow a mix of land uses that are compatible with the two zones being separated.

Transitions zones are the areas between regions where two distinct habitats coexist as one habitat transitions into another. Examples include the regions between forest types or in estuaries that are between salty oceans and freshwater rivers.

Our sense of betweenness remains largely unconsidered. We don't think about the act of transitioning and the meaning of those transitions. As a space and as a sense of transition, betweenness structures daily life as a continuous flow rather than a series of discrete moments by smoothing the seams.

I am using the concept of betweenness to explore the passage from one meaningful place or event to another. I want us to recognize that these moments of transition are also meaningful in their own right.

These transitions are meaningful because they open us up. Transitions place us in exposed and vulnerable positions. The phrase "between wind and water" referred to a part of the ship's side. It is the part of the ship which is alternately exposed to the elements and submerged in the water. This *between* place is a particularly dangerous place, for it is vulnerable to attack and corrosion. Our own moments of betweenness are equally exposed positions, vulnerable to attack and corrosion.

Our recognition of our sense of vulnerability is crucial. We all feel the anxiety of these vulnerable moments. We experience these moments as we walk into new environments or encounter new situations.

We haven't given ourselves the ability to acknowledge, recognize, and cultivate these *between* zones and embrace our sense of vulnerability. We haven't given ourselves places or periods where we willfully shift between various facets of our lives. When we drive to work, we have a zone between work and home that is our place that allows us to transition. Due to the immediate waves, the gaps *between* have been shrunk. Our sense of *between* is on the verge of disappearing altogether, as constant entanglement has become our new normal.

We need to understand how to listen to the waves and the spaces between the waves. We need to understand that part of our journey is to drift in and out of awareness of the waves surrounding us, recognizing the fiendish complexity of the patterns.

As previously noted, Aristotle and others considered it essential that that we maintain distance in order to allow ourselves the ability to develop our own sense of catharsis. When we cultivate betweenness, we cultivate the ability to find the distance necessary to address life.

CHAPTER 27

Dipping Your Bucket

Many drops make a bucket ...

—Percy Ross

*W*hile we carried enough food for the entire trip, each day we needed to find a water source in order to replenish our canteens. We dipped the bucket into a well and drew up pure, clean mountain water.

Our bucket filling was easy. It didn't take us much time. It didn't cost much money. Anyone of us could do it. Today, many of us only have to open a tap at any time of day or night to obtain as much clean water as we want.

This is not the case for a large percentage of the world. In many parts of the world, the search for water occupies a significant part of the day. As I wrote this, according to UNICEF, almost "37 per cent of the developing world's population—2.5 billion people—lack improved sanitation facilities, and over 780 million people still use unsafe drinking water sources."

Our mental water bucket

Our mental water buckets have the same problem, although with these buckets, it is never a question of half-full or half-empty. These buckets are always full. The question is, full of what?

Do we have ready access to an infrastructure that lets us safely draw as much mental water as we want on demand? Do we have inadequate access to safe water? Do we only have access to sanitation services that will sicken and possibly kill us? Can we open a tap at any time of day or night to obtain as much clean water as we want? Or are our minds drawing unsafe water?

A "clear" mountain stream can harbor all kinds of pollutants and bacteria. We can purify water through boiling, chemical treatments, or water filters. We can purify our minds through contemplation.

CHAPTER 28

Pulling Your Ropes

We cannot swing up on a rope that is attached only to our own belt.

—William Ernest Hocking

*A*s we set up camp each night, we pulled out our tents. We uncoiled our ropes. We looked for a flat place on which to set up. Pitching your tent isn't rocket science; however, it does take time and practice. If you pull the ropes too tight on one side, the tent will lean. If you leave the ropes too loose, the tent will not hold its shape. In short, pitching a tent is almost always about finding the right place and reconciling various competing rope tensions.

It seems to me that we all struggle in our contemplation to reconcile various competing internal pressures. We engage in a cognitive balancing act in order to pitch our mental tents. Without ever thinking about it, our brains pull the ropes that allow us to keep our mental tents stable and secure. With cultivated contemplation, we can think about how we can pull these ropes.

Clearly, this is not an original observation; I suspect that most of us have frequently felt those tugs and frequently felt many of these tugs simultaneously. These tugs of entanglement often conflict, and it is tough to reconcile all of the tensions.

For example, we want to be part of something while concurrently we want to stand apart as individuals. This is our struggle between community and individuality.

Or as another example, we want to engage in action while concurrently wanting to have time to contemplate. This is the struggle that Saint Augustine clearly laid out in his third way. And as a final example, we are torn on how to cultivate our entanglements and our ability to influence the erosion around us.

To quote Csikszentmihalyi, there are also the pulls that are found when we seek to attain great individual accomplishments as "we [also] risk being mired in self-centered egotism." Or if we focus "exclusively on integration [we] will be well connected and secure, but lack autonomous individuality. Only when a person invests equal amounts of psychic energy in these two processes and avoids both selfishness and conformity is the self likely to reflect complexity." Then the individual can become fully realized.

Contemplation gives us the ability to see the strings and pull the strings we choose. We must pull in constant, steady fashion so that we can lift and dip our mental buckets in a fashion that allows us to become fully engaged in life.

CHAPTER 29

Moving from Tribe to Community

We are in a community each time we find
a place where we belong.

—Peter F. Block

Our group was made up of Scouts from multiple troops. We had split off from our greater groups to come together for this trip out of a mutual sense of purpose. We became a small tribe. We knew that we would break apart once the journey was done. But we knew we would always have this journey in common. This journey would always entangle us; it would always connect us.

Maybe unintentionally—but definitely unknowingly—our hyperentangled community is breaking into a tribal culture. These tribes do not seem to ever truly connect with each other.

Our new world is composed of cultural niches, populated only with our own particular tribes. Our shamans are those who say what the members already think and reinforce the existing doxa. Immediate waves of jargon win over fact. Our hyperentangled society pushes us into our particular tribe and doxa. The problem is that we end up taking our truths only from the people we trust within our tribe, without acknowledging that all tribes are flawed in some fashion.

In many ways, we all drift toward tribalism. Tribalism is deeply engrained in our genetic makeup, evolutionary history, and biological heritage. As such, it is the easiest option to take.

Tribalism stems from the kin selection process. This process evolved over countless generations in response to the ever-present dangers to self and family. It results in the encouragement of adult members of the clan to sacrifice themselves, if necessary, for the survival of their own offspring and those of their siblings, and to have a bias to their particular tribe.

These small, homogenous groups have shared values which are remarkably strong and important. However, these small groups can be a nightmare of conformity.

Further, they can also be exceptionally dangerous to outsiders. The *other* is seen as unknown; the *other* is seen as dangerous; the *other* is seen as threatening. The *other* had to be either avoided or destroyed. Hannah Arendt, in *The Origins of Totalitarianism*, explained how the upsurge of tribal distinctions and hatreds of the *other* in Europe ultimately resulted in Fascism and Nazism.

It may be that as we blindly try to cope, we retreat from the vast number of erosive entanglements. We select a particular tribe. We default to a singular point of view and, in turn, isolate ourselves within that view.

We become tribal not because of a lack of choice. We become tribal because of an excessive, overwhelming amount of choice. Our vulnerability-induced fear produced by the immediate waves of these choices pulls us into a riptide. We retreat into a tribe because we don't want to drown. If we recognize, acknowledge, and cultivate the underlying waves of love, we can escape our fear. The *other* is not necessarily bad; the *other* is simply unknown.

Is it possible to achieve the cooperative advantages of a small group without having the group reflexively view outsiders as the *other*? I contend that it is possible through acknowledging and embracing a *fission-fusion* social structure as networked individuals.

Fission-fusion structures have recognized boundaries between and among groups but boundaries which are not absolute and impermeable. This process is similar to the process that happened when the Scouts gathered together for this journey; as the group formed, the group acted together and stopped acting together as needed. In a world that is ever more connected, ever more entangled, the ability for groups to come together for a specific purpose, act, and then separate is also ever increasing.

In a fission-fusion model, the group can fracture (fission) into subgroups. These groups act within and adapt to environmental or social circumstances. However, they remain linked—entangled—with the first group. They are always welcome to rejoin (fusion) with the primary group. However, in the course of their activities, they may fuse with another group and, in turn, separate from that group as well.

What are networked individuals? In the words of Rainie and Wellman from their book *Networked*, "This new world of networked individualism is orientated around looser, more fragmented networks. Networked individuals have partial membership in multiple networks and rely less on permanent memberships in settled groups." They move "among relationships and milieus," where they tap "into sparsely knit networks of diverse associates rather than relying on tight connections to a relatively small number of core associates." The "structured and bounded voluntary organizations are becoming supplanted by more ad hoc, open and informal networks of civic involvement and religious practice."

I think that this fusion-fission networked individual model is grounded in finding commonality and cultivated entanglement with others. We want to recognize our commonality and balance our own interests with the interests of others.

In *Centerlined*, I held that we focus on finding ourselves to the detriment of finding community. With books on pop psychology and a social media that fosters narcissism, we become absorbed by the immediate waves of the self vice the longer waves of the community. I grounded that discussion in the writings of Karl Popper, Jürgen Habermas, and Ken Wilber as they outlined three components in our view of the world:

- **I** – Subjective, self-consciousness, self-expression, ego
- **It** – Objective, science and technology, empirical forms, universal truths
- **We** – Commonality, worldviews, common context, mutual understanding

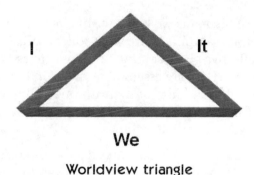

Worldview triangle

In *Centerlined*, I held that while "we have learned to differentiate between the three; we have gained an understanding of the 'I' and the 'It.' We have not learned how to allow development of the 'We.' We have not learned how to integrate the three. Much like a stool that requires three solid and uniform legs to be stable, our society needs three legs." One of the key things is to cultivate the development and integration of the third leg.

Contemplation helps you find those things that you truly hold in common with the others in this fission-fusion pattern of networked individuals. You can see your differences and still find common ground with all of the others you have become entangled with.

CHAPTER 30

Mirror, Mirror on the Wall

Life is a mirror and will reflect back
to the thinker what he thinks into it.

—Ernest Holmes

One of the items we knew we had to pack was a small, simple camping mirror. Made of highly polished metal or reflective glass, camping mirrors are essential items for all campers. They are essential because of their versatility; they are essential because of their unique ability to do multiple crucial functions. Campers can use them to start fires, to signal, or to do many other things.

Mirrors in life are so ubiquitous that we often forget their importance. From mirrors within telescopes that help us see the stars to mirrors that are used for signaling, mirrors come in all shapes and sizes. In some cases, mirrors filter out specific wavelengths, and in other cases, they alter reflected images.

However, the most common use is as a looking glass. A looking glass allows us to see and groom ourselves. How many times a day does each of us pass by a mirror and look at ourselves much as Narcissus looked at himself in the water?

We all have a mirror in our minds—a mirror that reflects, filters, and alters our mental images. While our mental mirror can perform external-facing functions, most commonly our mental mirror acts as a looking glass, reflecting ourselves back to ourselves in a highly self-absorbed fashion.

Self-absorption is a form of induced erosion and dooms our world to failure. Self-absorption gives us little or no capacity for listening, caring, or understanding the needs of others. Self-absorption leaves us without a true and intimate entanglement to others.

Our hyperentangled society fosters narcissism by only giving us enough distance to let us focus on the superficial short waves. We incessantly self-promote. We obsess on superficial uniqueness. Our blogs, our tweets, our social media pages, and our reality shows promote the most banal, ordinary, and unimpressive people as role models. We have a narcissistic society because we have created it.

The sad part is that the narcissists do not realize that they are narcissistic. In *The Narcissism Epidemic*, Twenge and Campbell conducted an extensive analysis of college students in order to identify the current level of self-involvement. The findings were fascinating. In 1982, 15 percent of sampled population scored high on the Narcissistic Personality Inventory; by 2006, the number had soared to 25 percent. In the 1950s, just 12 percent of respondents agreed with the statement "I am an important person." By the 1980s, 80 percent of the respondents felt special.

Balancing self-directed attention with other-directed attention is an important part of our development. While not uncommon for children to view themselves as the center of the universe, adults and societies need see beyond themselves.

Many of us aren't doing it very well. If the focus is on me, I can't cultivate the long and underlying waves and the loving relationships with others. If I am stuck in an adolescent self-absorption, how can I see beyond myself to the "We"? If it is all about me, then where is the space needed to recognize the *other*. Society needs to mature beyond the point of mental adolescence.

If our journey is to make any sense at all, it has to lead out and away from ourselves. It has to allow us to intersect with the paths of others, to cultivate the "We." It has to allow us to find commonality.

On this trail, the younger Scouts had to rapidly realize that it was not all about them. It was about this band, this community, and its attempt to cross the island. In order for one to finish, all had to finish. In order for all to finish, each had to finish as well. Self-absorption would doom us to failure.

CHAPTER 31

Not Seeking Badges and Gold Stars

To set the cause above renown, to love the game above the prize.

—Sir Henry John Newbolt

*T*he Scouts had knowledge of many of the skills necessary to survive and excel. They had received the badges. However, they still had to learn how to connect the skills with real life.

How many times have we met someone with all of the certificates and qualifications, only to realize that he or she couldn't do the job? How many times have we encountered someone who we thought couldn't satisfy the "requirements" but became an invaluable part of the team? How many times have we had spirited conversations with self-proclaimed experts who use their credentials and highly specialized knowledge of minutiae to steamroll discussions?

Badges and stars

We have focused on getting gold stars. In the short-term financial culture, the quarterly review culture, the testing culture, or simply the gaming culture, we are always looking for the next gold star.

The scorecards, badges, and gold stars routinely miss the mark. We are measuring and rewarding the wrong things. I am as guilty of this as everyone else. I love using scorecards to manage and show project status. Frequently, I have to adjust my expectations when my initial goals prove to be off the mark.

Life would be much, much simpler if the trophies and medals were our final expression. With them, we know the criteria and a defined destination. Life would be much simpler if we knew all of the criteria and had a defined destination. Life is not like that.

Gold stars or badges are not the reasons for our own journeys. Contemplation lets us see beyond the immediate and to toward the underlying.

CHAPTER 32

Making Waves

Complete peace equally reigns between two mental waves.

—Swami Sivananda

I started swimming on a regular basis again. Growing up on a lake, a summer day without a dip in the lake was a day wasted. Not all of us were great swimmers. Some were strong and sleek; others flailed and struggled.

The stronger swimmers gracefully cut through the water. They achieved fast results with minimal effort. The other swimmers chopped in the water. They made lots and lots of short waves. They expended much more energy than the strong swimmers and achieved fewer results.

Making waves

From the moment they first dipped their toes into the water, each of the swimmers chose to become swimmers. The stronger swimmers became stronger through concentration and practice. They practiced and perfected their strokes; they made the water their own. They chose to become stronger.

I have to come to realize that waves don't just happen to you. Waves also are what you make happen.

You can choose what types of waves to make in your life. You can choose to make short waves that erode. You can choose to make short waves that cultivate. You can choose to make long waves that erode. You can choose to make long waves that cultivate.

We have those same options in life. We can choose to dip our toes into the contemplative waters. We can choose to practice and perfect. We can choose to make it our own. We can choose to cultivate contemplation.

CHAPTER 33

Taking Alternative Trails

The Web's connections are not our connections.

—Nicholas Carr

*A*s the days passed by, we went farther and farther into the heart of the island. The trail markers became much more subtle and nuanced. Our pathfinders were those who had advanced land navigation and scouting training. Our pathfinders were hard-pressed to stay on the trail. Broken twigs and piled rocks became major reference points. We struggled to keep our bearings.

We struggled because we were not wandering down the trails that others had already gone over. We were wandering down our own paths. We were wandering down paths that were just the barest glimpse of a trail. We were finding our own way.

This is in striking contrast to those of us who have come to depend upon our GPS devices. These small, ubiquitous applications are routinely built into our smartphones and give us our exact position on a digital map. The feeling we get is one of certainty and security.

We love the feeling of certainty as we use a GPS. We love the feeling of certainty until that point in time—and it has happened to all of us—when the GPS starts to recalculate and then recalculates again. We find that our certainty and security founded on the digital pathways is misplaced.

Immediate waves, overwhelming vectors, and technology force us down a set path, a concrete digital freeway with limited off-ramps and rest stops. It doesn't allow us to see the smaller routes. To echo Arendt, if life is a fabric of actions and events, we have to avoid a "natural process" where homogeneity and conformity replace diversity and freedom.

Another problem with the immediate wave and overwhelming vectors is that we incorrectly associate understanding with factoids and sound bites with insights and knowledge. The clicks on hyperlinks and web searches lead us into an already-discovered country. The path is marked, algorithms guide us, the bridges are solid, and the mists have been digitally cleared. When we simply conduct searches of existing works, we lose the sense and joy of discovering on our own. We simply wander where others have gone before.

In the words of Tim Kreider, "Instant accessibility leaves us oddly disappointed, bored, endlessly craving more." It is good not have everything a mere click away because "learning how to transform mere ignorance into mystery, simple not knowing into wonder, is a useful skill."

My fear is that our fascination with the instantaneous entanglements that technology allows for us enables us to create faux entanglements. These entanglements only give us an illusion of understanding or community. We never truly engage or connect. These entanglements, in fact, only isolate us.

Contemplation allows us to break through these illusions.

CHAPTER 34

Seeing the Insights

*Ideas are not then genuine ideas unless they are tools
in a reflective examination.*

—John Dewey

After the day's hike and after the fire died, we stargazed. We waited for the various constellations to magically appear in the sky.

In our daily lives, we also wait.

Often, we wait without realizing it or realize what we are waiting for.

We wait for new insights. And insights matter. Insights are the culmination of our contemplative process.

I contend that the traditional pyramid of knowledge is incomplete. The traditional knowledge pyramid culminated in wisdom. I think that there is a level beyond that, and that step is insight.

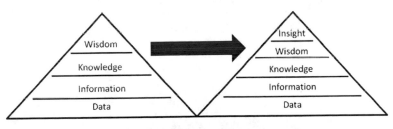

Insight pyramid

Insights are our glimpses into the underlying. Insights are those rare moments when we fully see the world.

Insights are not simply words, phrases, or thoughts. Insights don't end thought; insights begin thought. Insights are the result of embracing active contemplation. They give us the power to raise questions and foster understanding.

Insights come from listening. They come from trouble. They come from nature. Insights occur when the dissimilar intersect. For we seek the matter of the universe, invisible in the immediate waves, but at the core of our conscious experience.

Insights don't come about passively. They don't come from sitting on the sidelines or from playing an online game or from watching television.

Insights come from being awake. Insights occur when we are alert enough to actually notice. Insights come out of the corner of the eye, in the shower, or when we're not trying. Sometimes insights sneak in when we're half-asleep and too numb to be afraid.

Contemplation gives us the distance to find insights. By not dealing with the superficial appearance of experience, contemplation lets us find the insights to grasp the ensuring universal truths that lie below the immediate waves.

CHAPTER 35

Repacking

Your beliefs become your thoughts.
Your thoughts become your words.
Your words become your actions.
Your actions become your habits.
Your habits become your values.
Your values become your destiny.

—Mahatma Gandhi

I remember my first camping trip as a brand-new Scout. My brother and I took out our *Scout Handbook*. We went down the entire list. We found and packed everything on that list—everything.

Once we started, we thought that we had done something wrong. As we set up camp, we realized that we had done something wrong.

We had brought too much of one thing. We had not thought to bring other things. We had used the checklist as the definitive guide.

We thought that everything was necessary and equally important. We didn't know how to prioritize, how to discard, how to sort through the list to find the necessary items.

On the journey across the island, we wanted to prevent the same type of thing from happening. So we sorted through the backpacks before we started. We reviewed each item. We discarded many items. We included other items. Some of the backpacks were nearly emptied of extraneous items before we "properly" repacked them in order to accommodate our actual needs.

The physical items made a difference. Too many items could be an unnecessary burden. Too few could put us at a real risk. What we chose to carry, what we chose to keep, and what we chose to discard mattered a great, great deal. Everything within our packs mattered.

In life, we carry our mental backpacks. The mental items we carry make a difference. What we carry with us is influenced and shaped by the style and bias we all have. In order to repack, we have to recognize and acknowledge the different styles and biases that we all brought with us. We have to cultivate the styles and biases that we carry and shape them to what we want.

Cognitive styles are consistent patterns of behavior within a range of individual variability, our way of responding to and using stimuli, and how we process information, organize information, and prefer to learn. Our style is less about the decisions that we actually make and more about the processes we use to make them. Cognitive style is not about aptitude.

Our cognitive bias is our patterns in judgment and our instances of evolved mental behavior. We all have our own series of biases. Some are adaptive because they lead to more effective actions in given contexts or enable faster decisions when faster decisions are of greater value.

We each have a voice inside of us that is always "should-ing" us, telling us exactly how inept we really are, what we have failed at, what we are going to fail at, or where we need to bow down. None of us is immune.

The voice improves from a script based on our cognitive styles, our cognitive biases, the things we love, the things we fear, and all the things we've packed. The question is how do we respond to that voice? How do we actually come to

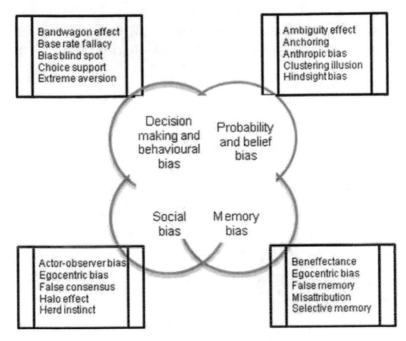

Bandwagon effect
Base rate fallacy
Bias blind spot
Choice support
Extreme aversion

Ambiguity effect
Anchoring
Anthropic bias
Clustering illusion
Hindsight bias

Decision making and behavioural bias

Probability and belief bias

Social bias

Memory bias

Actor-observer bias
Egocentric bias
False consensus
Halo effect
Herd instinct

Beneffectance
Egocentric bias
False memory
Misattribution
Selective memory

Types of cognitive bias

clearly hear that voice and fully understand why it is saying something to us?

It is not easy to clean out and repack your backpack, even if you understand the style, and the biases you brought with you. You packed it, and you want to cling to your belongings wherever you go. It is easy for us to get trapped in an echo chamber of the self and fail to adequately question our own assumptions.

If we are so caught in the immediate waves and let the strobe lights blind us, we will not have enough distance to properly respond to that one true, underlying voice. We will let the white noise clutter our thoughts. Through the cultivation of silence, solitude, and stillness, we can contemplate the contents of our backpacks; we can face our private logic and lifestyle and replace the pieces that no longer need to be part of our journey. We can choose our response.

CHAPTER 36

Entangling Intentionally

Society is commonly too cheap.

—Thoreau

Our small group quickly bonded. We were fortunate since we had all meet before and knew one another on some basic level.

Have you ever meet someone who immediately tried to put himself or herself completely and totally in your life, instantly becoming your best friend? Have you ever meet people who would not give you the time of day until they figured out how it could benefit them? Do you have friendships that have withstood time, that pick up where they left off regardless of the time and distance between the encounters?

What are healthy, meaningful, loving entanglements? In *Walden*, Thoreau remarked that we are often too much in contact with others and in ways that are random. He wrote that we cannot respect each other if we "stumble over one another." He believed that we are unable to acquire value for each other if there is not enough space between us.

How can we analyze the entanglement spectrum around us? We can look at the entanglements from a variety of perspectives. To simplify matters, I would put forward the following four paired categories. These categories are not binary in nature but rather exist on a spectrum. Further, they are representative and not exhaustive. Entanglements fall between the respective end points.

As we acknowledge and cultivate entanglements, we need to understand them so that the entanglements are intentional. Once we have done that, we repack our backpacks meaningfully.

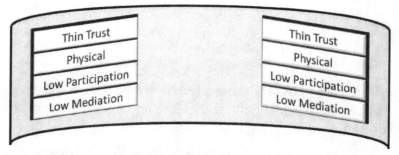

Types of entanglements

Between Thin and Thick Trust

Using the construct put forward by Robert D. Putnam in his book *Bowling Alone*, our entanglements are based in either thin or thick trust. To paraphrase Putnam, thin trust is social trust. It is the trust which extends beyond an individual's actual network. It extends beyond the tribe and into the doxa surrounding the *other*. It extends into a more implicit sense of common networks and assumptions of eventual reciprocity. Thin trust is based more on community norms than personal experience.

Thick trust is the trust embedded in personal relationships. These are linkages that are strong and frequent. For Putnam, thick trust is as strong as ever.

Conversely, in our current society, thin trust has become rarer. Our trust in the *other* to do the right thing simply because it is the right thing seems have to dropped. Our e-mail boxes become clogged with spam mail. We don't trust our politicians to act in the public's best interest. We don't believe that we can rely on our loose-knit communities to actually assist us.

Between Physical and Virtual

Beyond thin and thick trust, entanglements have a physical component to them. Relationships can be conducted across the spectrum of being completely online or being completely physical in nature.

In a world increasingly connected by technology, the newness and different nature of the virtual relationships can challenge us. The atemporal and aspatial nature of virtual relationships have a great appeal. It is easier to create a persona of who you want to be than it is to cultivate and nurture yourself to become that person. It is easier to text something negative and easier to "unfriend" someone than it is to actually talk with him or her to resolve an issue. The virtual relationships have a very transactional quality to them. Physical relationships require that you look someone in the eye and express what you really feel.

We all have relationships that extend across different physical and virtual dimensions. We have relationships in our social media networks. We have relationships in our workplaces. We have relationships where we see the other person frequently. We have relationships were see the other person very rarely. The question we face is how to recognize and acknowledge the nature of these entanglements and how we embrace them.

Between Low and High Participation

Participating is not merely showing up, Facebook liking, or sending in a check. Participation is something more than oneself; participation is beyond the needs of the ego.

We have to recognize that life is a team sport. We all play on a team. And participants are different than spectators.

You need to prevent the illusion of doing something by actually participating in something. And to participate is to understand that your presence matters. When you see something or hear something, your engagement and response is part of the event.

Between Low and High Mediation

For the first time in history, people are spending more hours of their days immersed in computer-mediated environments. Mediated entanglement addresses the issue that we have begun interpret our environment in a radically different fashion than in the past. We have shifted from the historically dominant "experiential reality," where we actually experienced something, to an "observational reality." We observe; we look toward representations of reality rather than having unfiltered experiences. This fundamentally transforms the way we recognize ourselves and reality.

As I've written before, we need understand our entanglements. We have to live in each and every moment. As each moment goes by, we should contemplate and embrace it.

CHAPTER 37

Crossing

What is great in man is that he is a bridge and not an end.

—Nietzsche

Given the terrain, each day we had to cross multiple and different types of bridges. Early on, the bridges were on major roads. They were sturdy and well reinforced. In short, they were exceptionally safe. We could cross in complete confidence, knowing that we would end up on the other side without issues.

All sorts of bridges in our lives

As we were taking the trail and going around the bends, we started encountering bridges that were significantly, shall we say, less established. The bridges were decades old, without maintenance. These bridges brought about challenges. We wondered if we could cross them. We wondered if we should cross them. But to continue on our journey, we had to cross them.

Once we'd crossed, we would look back. For many, we wondered why we had been so concerned in the first place. From the other side, it was clear how to cross. For others, we stared in amazement that we had been able to make it. Sometimes we crossed, realized that the path dead-ended, and had to turn around.

As big or as small as they were, the bridges were visible, physical. Often in life, our visible bridges have signs which warned us of something that may be ahead. With clear, direct guidance, such as "High Winds," "Toll Ahead," or "Freezes Before Road," we could anticipate what we were going to face.

Our mental bridges don't have that sense of clarity. Our internal crossings are not nearly as clear cut. An internal crossing could appear initially as a shaky structure. In fact, the internal cross was a solid, reinforced structure. We wonder why we worried and didn't take that stride earlier. What we thought of as a terrifying prospect turns out to be an illusion.

Conversely, what appeared to be a solid surface, a bridge could have eroded at its foundation and was about to collapse. We could only wonder about what caused the erosion.

In order to continue on the journey, we need to take contemplative strides and cross. As with seeing insights, our crossings frequently have to be taken in a single stride.

Our mental strides will transport us onto entirely new planes of insight only if we take them. What would appear to appear to an observer standing on one side as a terrifying chasm is to an observer on the other side a safe and modest step. On our journeys, contemplative strides will bring us surprising visions of the future and surprising visions of the past as we turn around and look back.

CHAPTER 38

Awakening Beauty

Beauty in things exist in the mind which contemplates them.

—David Hume

As we journeyed, we saw something emerge. The imposed silence, solitude, and stillness gave us enough distance to allow something to grow. With cultivated contemplation, we saw beauty emerge.

Most of life is neither sexy nor glamorous, but it can be beautiful. Beauty is not fleeting or self-absorbed. Glamour is. Glamour is found in the baubles of life; glamour is the cotton candy of food. Glamour is fleeting. Glamour is entertaining.

What is beauty? Beauty is not sexy. Beauty is not glamour.

Beauty is our perception of the underlying waves; beauty is our glimpse into the perennial. Beauty is realization of ideals, values, and vision. Beauty is found in art, in nature, in the other. Beauty produces inspiration. Beauty has permanence. Beauty engages.

Beauty impacts us through all of our senses. As Maritain says, beauty "delights the understanding."

Beauty is the realization of ideals, values, and vision and produces inspiration and adherence. While it can be pleasurable, beauty is not utilitarian.

Beauty calls us. It calls us to become; it calls us to transform.

Many have asked the question, what is beauty? Is beauty an intrinsic feature of the world or an aspect of our perceptions? Is beauty by design, or is it by nature? What makes us crave it so much? We live in a world that is full of extravagant beauty. We can find many instances of beauty just by *merely looking around*.

To paraphrase the words of the late John O'Donohue, what beauty can do is to call us to be something more than we could be if we are alone. It inspires us and feeds our senses. Beauty does not diminish us; rather, beauty makes us greater than we would be alone. Beauty is not imitative; beauty is creative. Beauty is not regressive; beauty is imaginative. Beauty is at the core of our conscious experience.

Contemplation gives us the distance to find beauty. When we are not caught in the immediate and superficial, we can see the underlying beauty of the world.

Awakening beauty is our response to those calls. Awakening beauty means that we create long waves that cultivate love.

In the words of O'Donohue, "To behold beauty dignifies your life; it heals you and calls you out beyond the smallness of your own self-limitation to experience new horizons. To experience beauty is to have your life enlarged."

Contemplation gives you enough distance to allow beauty to awaken. Contemplation allows you to listen to the voice of beauty. Through cultivation, through solitude, through stillness, through silence, we can awaken beauty in everyday life.

CHAPTER 39

Back to the Beginning

The beginning is always today.

—Mary Wollstonecraft Shelley

Back to the beginning

A week or so later, I returned to the exact same place where I had started before. It was with a different group and for a different purpose. We walked many of the same roads, but the meaning was not the same. My backpack was full of items, some different, some the same.

With contemplation, we can allow our life narrative to emerge from our personal experience and awareness rather than accept the narrative of a predetermined role from a script written long ago by others. We can choose.

With contemplation, we can reject the inauthentic narratives. We can reject doing what everybody else is doing simply because everyone else is doing it. We can swim through the short waves. We can see beyond the strobe lights. We can see the moon glow. We can find distance.

With contemplation, we can allow our authentic narratives to emerge. By realizing that our choices are free, we can make personal decisions based on meaningful evaluations.

By cultivating and gaining distance, we can guide ourselves using the steady current. We can engage.

Contemplative living encourages us to explore our styles, and biases. It is through our contemplation that we have insights into the depths of our inner truths. Through this contemplation we discover who we are, how we are called to be in the greater community, and what is truly important. We can awaken beauty.

By living contemplatively, we can untangle.

Sample Group Discussion Questions

Where can you start a journey? When? What actions do you need to take?

Are entanglements only driven by love or by fear? What other perennial truths could drive entanglements?

The framework and pillars of contemplation were a critical part of this book. What was missed? What was extraneous? Do they address everything you believe necessary?

Waves, lights, bypassing, and buckets were some of the metaphors used by the author for the actions necessary to cultivate contemplation. What other metaphors can you think of from your own life?

Can you think of an instance when you became entangled inadvertently? Who forced it upon you? How was it forced up you? How did you untangle yourself?

What moments in your life have you needed to cross a bridge that appeared to be unsound?

What things have you packed that you know you should take out of your mental backpack?

How often does your mental mirror reflect outward?

Where can you see the immediate, long, and underlying waves in your life?

Is the author's contention that insights are above wisdom valid?

It has been said that "truth is beauty, and beauty is truth." Is that a valid statement? How does that apply to the notion of contemplation set forth by the author?

Additional group discussion questions are available at www.untangledthebook.com

Selected Works Consulted

Arendt, Hannah. *Totalitarianism: Part Three of the Origins of Totalitarianism*. New York: Harcourt Brace Jovanovich, 1968.

Armstrong, Karen. *A History of God: The 4000-Year Quest of Judaism, Christianity and Islam*. New York: Alfred A. Knopf, 1993

Armstrong, Karen. *The Great Transformation: The Beginning of Our Religious Traditions*. New York: Alfred A. Knopf, 2006.

Arraj, James. *Mysticism, Metaphysics and Maritain*. Chiloquin, OR: Inner Growth Books, 1993.

Blank, Hanne. *Straight*. Boston: Beacon Press, 2012.

Behary, Wendy T. *Disarming the Narcissist*. Oakland, CA: New Harbinger Publications, 2003.

Blakeslee, Sandra and Matthew Blakeslee. *The Body Has a Mind of Its Own*. New York: Random House Trade Paperbacks, 2008.

Boorstein, Sylvia. *It's Easier Than You Think*. New York: Harper One, 1995.

Carr, Nicholas. *The Shallows: What the Internet Is Doing to Our Brains*. New York: W. W. Norton, 2010.

Cashwell, C. S., D. P. Bentley, and P. Yarborough. "The Only Way Out Is Through: The Peril of Spiritual Bypass." *Counseling and Values* 51 (2007): 139–148.

Cobb, John B. *The Structure of Christian Existence*. http://www.religion-online.org/showchapter.asp?title=1086&C=1130. Accessed April 26, 2007.

Csikszentmihalyi, Mihaly. *Flow: The Psychology of Optimal Experience*. New York: Harper Perennial Modern Classics, 2008.

Cutler, Hugh Mercer. "The Myopia of the Cultural Relativist." *Intercollegiate Review*, Fall 2002. http://hughcurtler.com/relativism.html. Accessed September 2011.

Dallmayr, Fred. *In Search of the Good Life*. Lexington: University Press of Kentucky, 2007.

Florida, Richard. *The Flight of the Creative Class*. New York: HarperCollins, 2005.

France, Peter. *Hermits: The Insights of Solitude*. New York: Saint Martin's Griffin, 1996.

Fukuyama, Francis. *Trust*. New York: Free Press Paperbacks, 1995.

Furedi, Frank. *Culture of Fear*. New York: Continuum, 2002.

Glassner, Barry. *The Culture of Fear*. New York: Basic Books, 1999.

Gurdon, E. "Contemplative Life." *The Catholic Encyclopedia*, vol. 4. New York: Robert Appleton Company, 1908. http://www.newadvent.org/cathen/04329a.htm. Accessed December 16, 2011.

Heath, Chip and Dan Heath. *Switch: How to Change Things When Change Is Hard*. New York: Broadway Books, 2010.

Hillman, James. *The Soul's Code: In Search of Character and Calling*. New York: Random House, 1996.

Iyengar, Sheena. *The Art of Choosing*. New York: Twelve, 2010.

John of the Cross. *Dark Night of the Soul*. Mineola, NY: Dover Thrift Edition 2003.

Katzenbach, Jon R. *Why Pride Matters More Than Money.* New York: Crown Business, 2003.

Kreider, Tim. "In Praise of Not Knowing." *New York Times,* June 19, 2011.

Lilly, John and E. J. Gold. *Tanks for the Memories.* Nevada City, CA: Gateways, 1995.

Look, Brandon C. "Gottfried Wilhelm Leibniz," *Stanford Encyclopedia of Philosophy (Fall 2008 Edition).* Edited by Edward N. Zalta. http://plato.stanford.edu/archives/fall2008/entries/leibniz/. Accessed December 31,2012

Marion, Jim. *Putting on the Mind of Christ.* Charlottesville, VA: Hampton Roads Publishing Company, 2000.

Merton, Thomas. *New Seeds of Contemplation.* New York: New Directions Books, New York, 1961.

Merton, Thomas. "Notes for a Philosophy of Solitude." *Disputed Questions.* New York: Farrar, Straus, and Cudahy, 1960. 177–207.

Morin, Edgar. *On Complexity.* Cresskill, NJ: Hampton Press, 2008.

Nussbaum ,Martha C. *The Fragility of Goodness: Luck and Ethics in Greek Tragedy and Philosophy.* Cambridge: Cambridge University Press, 2001.

O'Donohue, John. *Beauty: The Invisible Embrace.* New York: Harper Perennial, 2004.

Palmer, Martin. *The Jesus Sutras.* New York: Random House, 2001.

Picard, Max. *The World of Silence.* Witchita, KS: Eighth Day Press, 2002.

Pinker, Steven. *The Better Angels of Our Nature.* London: Viking Press, 2011.

Poulain, Augustin. "Contemplation." *The Catholic Encyclopedia*. New York: Robert Appleton Company, 1908. http://www.newadvent.org/cathen/04324b.htm. Accessed December 16, 2011.

Putnam, Robert D. *Bowling Alone: The Collapse and Revival of American Community*. New York: Simon & Schuster Paperbacks, 2000.

Rainie, Lee and Barry Wellman. *Networked*. Cambridge, MA: MIT University Press, 2012.

Randall, Lisa. *Knocking On Heaven's Door*. New York: HarperCollins, 2011.

Sachs, Jeffrey D., *The Price of Civilization*. New York: Random House, 2011.

Shirky, Clay. *Cognitive Surplus: Creativity and Generosity in a Connected Age*. New York: Penguin Press, 2010.

Sienkiewicz, Henry J. *Centerlined*. Indianapolis, IN: Dog Ear Publishing, 2006.

Teresa of Avila. *Interior Castle*. Mineola, NY: Dover Thrift Edition, 2007.

Turkle, Sherry. *Alone Together*. New York: Basic Books, 2011.

Wicks, Robert. "Friedrich Nietzsche." *Stanford Encyclopedia of Philosophy (Summer 2011 Edition)*. Edited by Edward N. Zalta. http://plato.stanford.edu/archives/sum2011/entries/nietzsche/. Accessed December 31, 2012

Zajonc, Arthur. *Meditation As Contemplative Inquiry*. Great Barrington, MA: Lindisfarne Books, 2009.

Acknowledgments

Each friend represents a world in us, a world not
possibly born until they arrive, and it is only
by this meeting a new world is born.

—Anaïs Nin

$\mathcal{W}$e have all been entangled by others, often in ways that go unrecognized. I have been very fortunate to have had many personal, professional, and intellectual entanglements in my life. Each one of them has caused a wave that rippled through me, and I hope that I have been able to make them proud as I have tried to incorporate those waves. It remains tough to thank everyone who has helped me, and I apologize for those I have omitted.

For the background theme, the Boy Scouts of the Taiwan district.

For the music that I continually played while writing, Ennio Morricone and the soundtrack to *The Mission*.

My profound thanks goes to all of those who read the galleys and put up with me as I wrote this: my friends and colleagues at the Defense Information Systems Agency; Federal Executive Institute; Moreau Seminary; the Arts Club of Washington; Amber Ortner, Megan Weddle, Adrienne Miller and the entire Dog Ear team; Roberta "Bobbie" Stemfley; Jackie Snouffer; Dr. Stephanie McMillan; Amy Mather; Dan Andeson; Denise Jennings; Kevin Broadwater and James Vaughn; Angie Berger; Maurice "Jay" Smith; Lisa Billingham and Jay Schober; Lorrie Manasse; Krista Tippett and the On

Being team; Kathy Beaver; David Still; Alicia Kennerly; Abi Conrad; Kimberly Chapman; Shelly Barber; Sandra Mascoll; Michael Higgs; Thomas Kowalevicz; Sharmaine Shorter; William Keely; Robert Gorman; Hillary Morgan; Myra Powell; Michael Sullivan and David Houle; Thomas Donohue; Robert Fulscher; Jason Spritzer; Joseph Beckish; Shawn Newman; Edward Renner; Robert Amato; Sune Andreasen; John Krause; Victor Vae'au; David Brooks; Alicia Murray; Michael Skelly; Francis James; Chang Shu-ling; Clark Murphy; David and Laurie Mastic; Carol Camp; Richard Adam; Brandon Schmittling; Kevin Clement; Ed Norwood; Amy Saidman; Amy Wilson; Linus Barloon; Brad Hatcher and Matt Speilman; Aaron Lippold; Andrew Wonpat; Robert Eisenhauer; Alma Miller; John Wasko; Phyllis Andes; Eileen Hamby; Russell "Rusty" Wilson; Patrice Wilmot; Marie Wyrma; Dennis and Cindy Moran; Richard Guther and Edward Shaw; Steve Clemmons and Andrew Oros; Anthony Levensalor; Mark and Susan Orndorf; Martin Gross and Kendra Altman; David Bullock; Nathan Maenle and Ariel Datoc; Warren Coats and Victorino (Ito) Briones; David Jones; Alfred Rivera; Michael Gordy Bob Sacheli; Bill Gleich; Chase Maggiano; Ben Carver; Will Bower; Kevin Wells; Scott Mendenhall; Carter, Jennifer, Dorothy and Sarah Lane; Douglas Yu and Sophie Miller; Andy and Marlene Tucker; Rob Lalumondier; Daniel Schneider and Emily Hellmuth; Dorinda Smith; Doug Dixon; Corey Rooney and Maureen Collins; Jason DeMoranville; Ben, Diane, and Christian Brady; Florence and Mel Anderson; Nelson and Jean Ehinger; Pat Neary; Roberta and Charlie Osborn; Florence and Ed Wallace; Julia, Charlotte, Maddy, Grace, Kayden, Maeve, Robert, John, Elise and Kim, my parents, and Jeffrey Brady.

My deepest gratitude goes to my family and friends. They have inspired me, challenged me, forced me to look at myself, and helped me to grow.

Index

About the Author

*A*n Eagle Scout, Henry J. Sienkiewicz has served in multiple positions within the United States Federal Senior Executive Service since 2008. His previous experience was as the founder and chief executive officer for Open Travel Software, an award-winning software developer focused on the global travel community, and in the chief information officer role at three technology companies. He or his companies have been the recipient of multiple awards for innovations or achievement in the technology industry. He retired as a United States Army Reserve lieutenant colonel in July 2008.

Henry holds a bachelor of arts from the University of Notre Dame and a master of science from Johns Hopkins University. He is also a graduate of the United States Army Command and General Staff College.

In 2006, he completed and published his first book, *Centerlined*, which dealt with interpersonal and organizational dynamics.

Henry resides in Alexandria, Virginia.

Disclaimer

As with my previous book, it goes without saying that the views expressed here represent my views and do not necessarily represent the views of any organization with which I am affiliated.

Book Orders

Untangled can be ordered online through Amazon (www.amazon.com), Barnes & Noble (www.bn.com), or directly from the author (www.untangledthebook.com).